CASE STUDIES IN
CULTURAL ANTHROPOLOGY

GENERAL EDITORS

George and Louise Spindler

STANFORD UNIVERSITY

THE VICE LORDS

Warriors of the Streets

Vice Lords

Warriors of the Streets

Keiser

CENGAGE
Learning

Australia • Brazil • Japan • Korea • Mexico • Singapore • Spain • United Kingdom • United States

CENGAGE
Learning™

Vice Lords: Warriors of the Streets

Keiser

Executive Editor:
Michele Baird

Maureen Staudt

Michael Stranz

Project Development Editor:
Linda de Stefano

Senior Marketing Coordinators:
Sara Mercurio

Lindsay Shapiro

Production/Manufacturing Manager:
Donna M. Brown

PreMedia Services Supervisor:
Rebecca A. Walker

Rights & Permissions Specialist:
Kalina Hintz

Cover Image:
Getty Images*

For product information and
technology assistance, contact us at **Cengage Learning Customer & Sales Support, 1-800-354-9706**

For permission to use material from this text or product, submit all requests online at **cengage.com/permissions** Further permissions questions can be emailed to **permissionrequest@cengage.com**

ISBN-13:   978-0-534-96931-8

ISBN-10:   0-534-96931-3

Cengage Learning
5191 Natorp Boulevard
Mason, Ohio 45040
USA

Cengage Learning is a leading provider of customized learning solutions with office locations around the globe, including Singapore, the United Kingdom, Australia, Mexico, Brazil, and Japan. Locate your local office at: **international.cengage.com/region**

Cengage Learning products are represented in Canada by Nelson Education, Ltd.

For your lifelong learning solutions, visit **custom.cengage.com**

Visit our corporate website at **cengage.com**

Printed in the United States of America

Foreword

About the Series

These case studies in cultural anthropology are designed to bring to students, in beginning and intermediate courses in the social sciences, insights into the richness and complexity of human life as it is lived in different ways and in different places. They are written by men and women who have lived in the societies they write about and who are professionally trained as observers and interpreters of human behavior. The authors are also teachers, and in writing their books they have kept the students who will read them foremost in their minds. It is our belief that when an understanding of ways of life very different from one's own is gained, abstractions and generalizations about social structure, cultural values, subsistence techniques, and the other universal categories of human social behavior become meaningful.

About the Author

Lincoln Keiser first developed an interest in black ghetto culture while working as a caseworker for the Cook County Department of Public Aid in 1962–1963. His assignment to a caseload in a predominantly black neighborhood on Chicago's West Side brought him into first-hand contact with ghetto life. During this time he gathered the material for *Hustler! The Autobiography of a Thief* (1965)—the life history of a small-time criminal who operated on the streets of one of Chicago's black ghettos. During 1964–1965 Dr. Keiser worked as a court caseworker in Boys Court North, a Chicago Municipal Court, and through this work first met members of the Vice Lords.

Dr. Keiser's first anthropological training came as an undergraduate at Lawrence College. Later he undertook graduate work at Northwestern University, and received an M.A. in anthropology in 1964. He recently conducted field research in the Hindu-Kush Mountains of northeastern Afghanistan, and wrote his Ph.D. thesis at the University of Rochester on a comparison of social control in two Afghan societies. He is presently teaching social, political, and urban anthropology at Wesleyan University.

About the Book

Though other case studies in the series had dealt with minority groups or communities in contemporary American society, this was the first to report on an urban subgroup. This description of the Vice Lords, a Chicago youth gang that is the subject of this case study, holds good in some degree for most gangs of similar age and composition, irrespective of ethnic identification, that operate in the depressed areas and ghettos of large American cities. Delinquent and criminal behavior and violence are patterned in the way of life of these gangs. Within the gang these behaviors are seen not only as acceptable, but as desirable, since they provide status for the organization and for its members, where other means to status achievement are blocked. These patterns of behavior and their supporting ideology can be understood as instrumental adaptations for survival in a desperate environment. Lincoln Keiser reports them objectively, in the ethnographic mood.

This study contributes to understanding phenomena beyond the specifics of a gang of "delinquent" youth in similar urban environments. Some of what is to be learned from case studies of this kind is applicable to a larger and growing segment of American life, for our culture has always included patterns for violence and criminality and these patterns have been accentuated by recent events. The understanding of criminality and violence in both their systematized and random forms and their social, cultural, and economic bases is of the greatest urgency in our time. Keiser's description of Vice Lord behavior is relevant to this larger problem.

Many more studies done in the vein of the ethnography and as much in the tradition of the participant-observer as possible must be carried out, and quickly, if the potential contribution of anthropology to the understanding of the urban environment is to be realized.

Fieldwork Edition

In this edition of *The Vice Lords*, we have included a new chapter on fieldwork from *Being an Anthropologist: Fieldwork in Eleven Cultures*, edited by G. Spindler. We think that adding this chapter to the case study to which it pertains truly enhances this volume. Ethnography is incomplete without more of the fieldwork experience, from a personal as well as methodological point of view, than is usually available. Lincoln Keiser's fieldwork experience is particularly notable. It is in an urban context, one in which a steadily increasing number of anthropologists are working. And it is a context where problems of entré, rapport, and even personal safety are of special importance.

Though included in this volume as Chapter 7, in order to avoid disrupting the orderly beginning of the case study or its flow, this chapter on fieldwork may be read with profit as an introduction to the case study, as well as a follow-up. Read in any order, the new material will increase comprehension of the anthropological enterprise as well as of the Vice Lords as a social system with a working ideology.

GEORGE AND LOUISE SPINDLER
General Editors

Calistoga, California
1978

Preface

The Vice Lord Nation is a large federation of street-corner groups whose home is the streets, alleys, and gangways of Chicago's major Black ghettos. Groups such as the Vice Lords—generally called delinquent gangs—are a popular subject for both the urban press and social scientists of various disciplines. In reading the scientific and popular literature on delinquent gangs one finds little attempt to provide a clear picture of the social and cultural systems of these groups. The aim of the press is to report news, while that of many sociologists and social psychologists interested in delinquent gangs is to construct theories explaining delinquent behavior. However, all groups and associations have structure, systems of organizations, and sets of commonly held values, and it is apparent from the hints found in the academic and popular literature that the so-called deviant or delinquent groups are no exception to the general social rule. What we classify as delinquency is only a part of a larger behavioral system, and if we are going to understand it, we have to understand the system as a whole. Thus, a study of a delinquent gang in its own right seemed worth the effort. I chose the Vice Lords for two reasons: the Vice Lords were reputed to be one of the largest and best-organized delinquent gangs in Chicago; and by chance I was able to establish a friendship with several Vice Lords who were willing to help with the research project. The first part of the research consisted solely of work with informants. It was conducted in 1964–1965 while I was employed by the Social Service Department of the Municipal Court of Chicago. In the summers of 1966 and 1967, after graduate training in social anthropology, I conducted field research in the Lawndale area of Chicago's West Side ghetto with a subgroup of the Vice Lords known as the City Lords. Through a Vice Lord I had known previously, I approached the leaders of the club, explained that I wanted to write a book about the Vice Lords, and offered to share any royalties with the club. The proposal was put before the club in a meeting and a majority of the members gave their approval.

The major purpose of this book is to provide a systematic description of the Vice Lord way of life. Actually constructing such a description, however, presents difficulties. In any field study an anthropologist observes wide variations in behavior that must be organized and interpreted in written form. In this study, culture and social system are basic organizing concepts. There are many ways to define these concepts, and the definitions used in this study are not necessarily the only correct ones. However, they did prove useful to me in making sense out of the wide behavioral variations I observed in Vice Lord life. The definitions of culture and social system provided by Clifford Geertz are followed in this study.

One of the more useful ways—but far from the only one—of distinguishing between culture and social system is to see the former as an ordered system of meaning and symbols in terms of which social interaction takes place; and to see the latter as the pattern of social interaction itself. . . . On the one level there is the framework of beliefs, expressive symbols, and values in terms of which individuals define their world, express their feelings, and make their judgements; on the other level there is the ongoing process of interactive behavior, whose persistent form we call social structure. Culture is the fabric of meaning in terms of which human beings interpret their experience and guide their action; social structure is the form that action takes, the actually existing network of social relations. Culture and social structure are then but different abstractions from the same phenomena. The one considers social action in respect to its meaning for those who carry it out, the other considers it in terms of its contribution to the functioning of some social system (Geertz 1957: 33–34).

Rather than give examples here from my observations of the behavior of the Vice Lords to illustrate these concepts, I will let my applications of them in the case study following speak for themselves.

However, it must be granted that the terms "culture" and "social system" are abstractions. They help the anthropologist to organize his observations. I have attempted to enliven the analysis and bring it closer to the reality of life among the Vice Lords by providing anecdotal observations of specific situations, events, and people. My observations, my selection of anecdotes, and surely my interpretations of what I saw and heard are consistently colored by my own biases, known and unknown. In order to provide some correction for these biases, I have turned to an individual, who sees the events, people, and situations I have described from an outsider's point of view, from the inside. In the last section of this book, after the culture and the social system of the Vice Lord Nation have been described, we shall view the Vice Lord world from the standpoint of the individual actor through the means of autobiography of one named Cupid.

It is impossible to adequately describe Vice Lord life without designating individuals by name. For their protection, therefore, no one has been designated by his real name. However, the names have not been made up by me, but are those actually used by members of the Vice Lords and other rival groups.

This book could not have been written without the help of others. I owe my greatest thanks to my wife Lynn for her constant encouragement and suggestions. I also profited from criticisms made by the faculty and graduate students of the Department of Anthropology, University of Rochester, and other friends. Specifically, thanks are owed to Marie Asnes, Warren Barbour, Dan Bauer, Arnold Green, Jane Guyer, David Jacobson, Sue Jacobson, Ghislane Lecours, Karl North, March Plume, Charles Scruggs, and George Scruggs, all of whom read and criticized various parts of the manuscript. Naturally, however, I bear all responsibility for the final version of the work.

R. Lincoln Keiser

Middletown, Conn.

Contents

Vice Lord Development

BEFORE BEGINNING OUR DISCUSSION of the Vice Lords' social and cultural system, it would be useful to look at the origin and subsequent growth of the group. The Vice Lords originated and have become differentiated and elaborated in an extremely short time. The "facts" presented in later chapters will make more sense if viewed against the background of Vice Lord development.

The description in this chapter is not presented as "historical fact." My aim is not to describe what happened, but what Vice Lords believe happened, for these beliefs affect Vice Lord behavior in the present. The data were gathered from a number of informants, and their accounts did not always completely correspond. Nevertheless, there was general agreement about broad lines of development.

It is generally stated that the Vice Lord Nation—referred to by Vice Lords as a "club," not a gang—originated in 1958 in what is usually called "Charlie Town," the Illinois State Training School for Boys at St. Charles, Illinois. In St. Charles the inmates live in what are called "cottages." The Vice Lords began in Harding Cottage, which housed the toughest boys in the institution. The club was started in the Lawndale area of Chicago in the fall of 1958, following the release of several members.

Lawndale has long been a breeding ground for "delinquent" groups primarily organized for fighting. Even before the area became predominantly Black, Polish and Jewish groups in Lawndale engaged in fierce gang fighting. (Short 1963:xxvi) After the area changed from White to Black, the fighting-gang pattern was continued by Black groups. One of the early Black fighting gangs in Lawndale was called the Clovers. At the time the Vice Lords first returned to Chicago from St. Charles, the Clovers were breaking up. Its members were getting older (approaching 20), and the group came under increasingly heavy pressure from a newer club called the Egyptian Cobras.

The Cobras had originally started in the Maxwell Street open-market area of Chicago's Near West Side known as "Jew Town." Later, a branch of the Cobras was initiated in a part of the West Side ghetto to the west of the Clovers called "K-Town" (because all the street names begin with K), and therefore this particular branch was called the K-Town Cobras. The K-Town Cobras soon increased in power and came into conflict with the older, more established Clovers. A boy living in the Clovers neighborhood who later became an important member of the Vice Lords tells the following story about the gang war between the Cobras and the Clovers:

> See, there was this humbug [fight] between the Clovers and the Egyptian Cobras. A boy got killed in that humbug. A Clover, a stud named Walker, got his head burned [shot] off with a shotgun, Jack! See, the Clovers, they was pretty old then. They had been out a long time, and they had their name. But the Cobras had just come out that summer [1957] in K-Town. And they started to fight the Clovers. The Clovers, they were established. They had their reputation. Now if the Cobras had fought them a couple of years before, they couldn't have done nothing with them. But by then all the Clovers were old and tired. So the Cobras hurt them, and that's when the Cobras first got their name.

In the fall of 1958 the members of the newly created Vice Lords moved into a section of the Clovers' old neighborhood vacated during the decline in Clover power. At this point there is a major divergence between accounts. One informant stated that many of the original members of the Vice Lords had previously belonged to a group known as the Imperial Chaplains located to the east of the Clovers. When the members of the Vice Lords returned to Chicago, they decided to start their own branch of the Imperials called the Imperial Vice Lords. The Imperial Vice Lords did not remain a branch for long. Friction developed between the two groups, and fighting broke out at a party at which both were present. Although the Lords were outnumbered, they won the fight, injuring several Imperials in the process. This established the Vice Lords as a group completely independent of the Imperials, and from then on the club was known as the Conservative[1] Vice Lord Nation.

Another informant told a different story. He said that the Vice Lords never were a part of the Imperial Chaplains. When the members of the Lords returned to Lawndale from St. Charles, they decided to continue the group as a small club organized for social (sponsoring parties) purposes. The original Lords had been members of many different fighting gangs—the Apaches, the Thunderbirds, the Golden Hawks, the Vampires, and the Imperial Chaplains. At first the club's activities consisted solely of giving parties, and hanging together. Slowly, the group grew until, almost inevitably, fighting developed with both the Cobras to the west in K-Town and the Imperial Chaplains to the east. It is my feeling that this latter version is probably closer to the actual fact, since (1) it is corroborated by other accounts; and (2) the informant who gave the account actually took part in this period of the group's development. The earlier version came from a Vice Lord who was in St. Charles during this time, and who was repeating stories told to him.

The first big jump in Vice Lord membership came from an alliance with a club called the El Commandoes. The El Commandoes was later completely absorbed by the Vice Lords. Like the early Vice Lords, the El Commandoes was primarily a

---

[1] Conservative refers to a reserved manner of dressing and acting.

social rather than a fighting group. Cave Man, one of the original Lords from St. Charles (and reputed by some to be the actual founder of the club), had previously been a member of the El Commandoes. When he returned to Lawndale, the alliance was made between the two groups. At first Cave Man's mother allowed the club to use the basement of her house for meetings and parties, but after several fights, the group was forced to give its parties in small rented halls and other basements. At parties such as these the group giving the affair furnishes something to drink, often a weak punch, and charges a small admission fee of 25 or 50 cents. The group usually makes a small amount of money which is used to finance future parties.

Social groups organized by a small group of friends to give parties are common in the Black ghettos of Chicago, and most do not develop into large federations of street-corner groups. That the Vice Lords developed in this direction can, I feel, be attributed to the power vacuum created by the decline of the Clovers. As the Cobras to the west, and the Imperial Chaplains to the east grew in strength, pressure was exerted on unorganized boys living in the Clovers' territory. This pressure consisted of shakedowns, demands that nonaffiliated individuals join one of the two groups, attempts to monopolize girls in the neighborhood, and fights and threats against the unorganized boys. It was probably inevitable that some group would become the rallying point for resistance against this pressure.

The Vice Lords became the rallying point following two incidents. The first began at a dance at which both Vice Lords and Cobras were present. During the course of the evening a Vice Lord and a Cobra argued over a girl. At the time the argument was considered inconsequential, but later, it took on major importance. Following the dance the Vice Lords went to a restaurant and by chance met a group of Cobras. The Vice Lords were wearing their special club capes, and each boy had an earring in one ear. The curiosity of the Cobras was aroused, and when the Vice Lords were asked why they were dressed in this manner, they explained it was the uniform of their new club. At first the Cobras suggested that the Vice Lords merge with them, but this offer was refused, and the Cobras decided to fight. The excuse the Cobras used was the argument that had taken place at the dance. The Cobra who had first been involved recognized the Vice Lord he had argued with and began to insult him. The Vice Lord, a boy named Bird (who later became supreme war counselor) hit the Cobra with a chair, which started a fight between the two groups. The Vice Lords claimed that the Cobras were not able to win—which may, or may not, be true. In any case the Vice Lords' claim that they had evenly matched the Cobras was the story spread throughout their neighborhood.

The second incident took place at a dance given by the Imperial Chaplains. Following is a Vice Lord's account of this incident:

> There was only a few of us there at this dance, and the Imperials, they jumped on [jump on, beat up] us for something, and this was when we first started fighting them. Like I said, there wasn't very many of us, but we made such a good fight at this showing that our name went out. See, a lot of the Imperials got hurt, and there was just us few. That's where we got our rep [reputation] from . . . you know, when we're outnumbered and still whupping ass.

After these incidents more individuals in the neighborhood joined the group and it grew to about 25 members. The original members still felt, however, that the club should remain primarily a social group. Their feelings began to change after the Cobras delivered a threatening message that the Lords had "only one more night left to live." Soon after, when several Imperial Chaplains broke into the basement of Cave Man's house (still used for club meetings), tore the furniture apart, and set fire to the basement, many of the Vice Lords decided that some kind of retaliation was necessary. A meeting was called to decide on a course of action. While many members did not feel the club was strong enough to fight either the Imperial Chaplains or the Cobras, a few of the more influential leaders had decided that the group could no longer remain simply a social club. According to one of the Lords present at this meeting:

> Everybody said, "Man, what can we do . . . against clubs as large as the Cobras and the Imperials?" So Bird said, "Well, one thing we can do is when we get ready to come down on any club, we send twenty guys home—tell them to go anywhere—watch TV. The five of us left will come down with guns, and after we shoot up a couple of studs we'll go back to our neighborhood and go home. We won't stay there and fight, we'll just go home . . . period! And when they come back through our neighborhood, they won't find nothing. We got to stop them from hurting us. We can't go on like this." So that's what we decided to do.

At this point in the Vice Lords' development, there was no institutionalized formal organization. There were no formal leadership positions and no formally recognized cleavages within the group. However, there were recognized leaders whose power stemmed from personal charisma. These leaders recognized that if the Vice Lords were to withstand both the Cobras and the Imperial Chaplains, they would have to increase their membership, for only with a larger group could they (1) control their neighborhood and thus protect themselves from surprise attacks; and (2) more evenly match their opponents in gang-fighting encounters.

The Vice Lords approached the task of recruiting new members in several different ways. Both the non-affiliated boys and other existing small clubs were potential sources of new members, but each posed different problems in recruitment. The methods used to recruit nonaffiliated boys were explained to me as follows:

> What we did, we did a survey of the neighborhood. We found out that there was fellows that was not accepted by any club for one reason or another—maybe a guy was disliked 'cause he had jumped on somebody, or because he wouldn't join some club. So we approached him from a different angle. First, instead of trying to scare him into becoming a part of our group, we tried to gain his friendship. See, what a lot of clubs didn't realize is that if a guy's your friend, he automatically be with you in a humbug [fight]. But what they would come through with, "You either join our club or we'll do this or we'll do that." We didn't do that. We said, "Well . . . ah . . . the Imperials are falling down on us, the Cobras are falling down on us. We got to do something about this, man! We can't keep being abused by these clubs. What we going to do, we going to get together and look out for our hoods [neighborhoods]."
> Now see, by him being tight with us, when the Cobras or the Imperials fall down on us, they going to fall down on him too. By making him our friend, automatically we make him the enemy of the other group. He only have one support, and that's to stay within the body that's with him.

Different tactics were necessary in recruiting new members from the smaller clubs located in various West Side neighborhoods. Many of these clubs were engaged in gang wars with stronger rivals. The Vice Lords supported these groups in their wars, and in return these clubs became subgroups of the Vice Lords. In other instances the Vice Lords entered alliances with groups which were also under pressure from the Cobras and Imperials, and slowly these groups began to consider themselves Vice Lords. According to my informants, a club called the Spanish Counts, with about twenty to twenty-five was absorbed into the Vice Lords in this manner. Although this club was small, several Spanish Counts had well-known gang-fighting reputations, and the Vice Lords' prestige was enhanced by the addition of these members.

Following the alliance with the Spanish Counts, the Vice Lords began a systematic attack on a club called the Imperial Knights, a group located between the Imperial Chaplains and the Cobras. While this group had previously refused all overtures for an alliance with the Vice Lords, the combined strength of the Spanish Counts and the Vice Lords was now too great for them, and finally, after a prolonged period of gang warfare, they agreed to become Vice Lords.

Possibly these various clubs would not have successfully merged if it had not been for intensified pressure from both the Cobras and Imperials. Both these groups renewed their threats to crush the Vice Lords, and began an all out attack. By this time it was too late. The addition of new members gave the Vice Lords added strength, and the increased prestige of the group continued to bring in new members—many with established gang-fighting reputations. In talking about this stage in the club's development one of my informants gave the following account, which reads something like the catalog of warriors in the Iliad:

> From the Imperial Knights we got guys like Fresh Up Freddie, Wade, Lil' Bull, Pole Cat, Napoleon, Goat, Duck; from the Clovers we got Cherokee, Prince G.G., Peanut, Hawk, and the Satisfier; from the Camancheroes came Sonny Boy Brown, Willy B., Blinkey; and from the Braves came Carlos, Zenith, and Blue Goose. Now all of these guys had reputations all around the West Side, and when other guys got together you could hear them talk about it. You could walk past (because they didn't know whether you was a part of the Vice Lords or not), and you'd hear them say, 'Those Vice Lords got some terrible guys in they group. You going to have to put up some strong resistance to stop them!'

Even with this increase in strength, however, the Vice Lords would have been at a definite disadvantage if the Cobras and the Imperials had been able to cooperate successfully. During a battle with the Vice Lords, however, the brother of the Cobras' president was accidentally shot by an Imperial, and a gang war between the Cobras and the Imperials resulted. This placed the Vice Lords in an advantageous position, since the Cobras now blamed Vice Lord attacks on the Imperials, while the Imperials blamed them on the Cobras.

In 1962 the Imperials began to break up, and from then on were less of a threat to the Vice Lords. In contrast, the war with the Cobras intensified, and in 1961 and 1962 flared out in numerous battles in which members of both clubs were killed. This is how a Vice Lord describes one of the early battles in the war with the Cobras:

One night we really found out whether or not we was ready. Almost every Cobra from the South Side, down Jew Town way, K-Town, and some of the King Cobras from the North Side all came over to the YMCA. We was in the gym playing ball—there was about fifty of us in there. They had gave what is called a bunking party. All the fellows would come over, play sports, eat, and at night they'd lock the doors and you'd sleep there. So both the Cobras and our fellows was there. And Lil' Herk in our club and Lil' Herk in the Cobras, they got to arguing about something that happened between them and a broad. So Herk said, "Well, man . . . I don't want to see all the fellows fighting, so what we'll do, me and you just go." So they took they shirts off, and they got ready to humbug. But Crazy Horse, they president, he came over and said, "No! If one Cobra fight, we all fight!" And Rico, he was in there at the time. Rico was one of the original seven in the Lords. So when the fight starts, Rico and Crazy Horse took over the picture, and everybody stop—just watching them, more or less. But when the real force of the Cobras come up from downstairs to fight, that's when the humbug really broke out. See, we got the best of that fight 'cause really, the Cobras that had they guns was stuck outside because the door was locked and they couldn't get in.

Following the growth in the Vice Lords' membership, there was a corresponding institutionalization in organization: (1) groups of Vice Lords from various parts of the West Side formed into distinct subgroups called "branches" which were joined in a loosely knit federation; (2) within each·branch leadership became institutionalized in specific positions; (3) age categories were set up which crosscut the branches; and (4) within branches, particular groups were given specific duties. We have already mentioned that many of the smaller clubs which the Vice Lords absorbed became distinct branches. In other instances groups of Vice Lords occupying neighborhoods some distance from the club's core territory also became separate branches. Following the establishment of branches, the original group centered at 16th and Lawndale became known as the City Lords, since they controlled that portion of the club's territory called Vice Lord City. Other important branches were: the Monroe Lords on Monroe Street, the Maypole Lords on Maypole Avenue, the California Lords, the Sacramento Lords, the 5th Avenue Lords, and the Albany Lords.

Within each branch, and for the club as a whole, leadership was institutionalized in positions. This development was a conscious response by the Vice Lords to the high probability that particular leaders would be arrested. The police approach to the problems posed by fighting clubs is to jail the leaders in hopes that the group will then dissolve. The Vice Lords solved this problem by developing leadership positions which provided an effective mechanism for replacing leaders jailed by the police. With the Vice Lords' newly gained size, there were many boys with leadership ability, and when a particular leader was arrested, another individual was chosen to occupy the vacated position.

Each branch was subdivided into age groupings called "Seniors," "Juniors," and "Midgets." In some branches there were even "Pee Wee" Vice Lords. Many of these formed particular subgroups within branches, each electing their own set of officers. In other instances these were social categories rather than functional groups. The age criteria of these groupings varied from branch to branch, and in any case were never completely rigid.

Writing the club name on a wall.

Branches were further subdivided into what I call cliques, some of which were entrusted with particular responsibilities. These groups were composed of a small number of individuals who "hung" together. An example of a clique entrusted with a specific responsibility is the Spy Patrol. This group never took part in gang fighting, but watched other clubs' activities, and reported what they saw to the president of the City Lords. At the time I did my research the Spy Patrol was no longer functioning, and my informants were not able to give more specific details about this group.

In 1962 the war with the Cobras reached its peak, and then began to wane. This was due to a variety of factors. The YMCA, through its detached worker program, was successful in reaching leaders of both the Vice Lords and the Cobras, and detached workers were often able to head off gang fights. Further, Black Nationalism began to influence boys in each group, and this acted as a check on gang fighting. According to several informants, after the sniper killing of a Black high school student in South Lawndale, a predominantly Polish neighborhood, both Vice Lords and Cobras united in retaliatory raids. Following is a Vice Lords account of this particular incident:

What happened, this guy was coming from school and he was shot and killed. It was in a gray hood [White neighborhood]. There was mostly Polish living over there. I guess they killed him 'cause he was a Negro. He wasn't doing nothing, just walking down the street coming from school . . . with two other studs. And the Man [the police] didn't know who did it. Anyway, he say he didn't. I guess it could have been anybody in the hood.

And when this happened . . . well, I don't know just exactly how it was, but everybody just thought the same way. The Lords decided to go on over there, and some kind of way we ended up with the Cobras too. It was just that everybody was out there, all the groups on the West Side. And we went through the high school over there, and the neighborhood every day and every night after that! And we dusted everybody we saw, Jack—tearing up property—we turned over cars—we did everything!

You know, before that, any time we went over there—in South Lawndale—we almost always would get dusted, or maybe even killed. But now they think twice . . . especially the older people because they have more at stake. Now you get some young studs, they might do it. You always got fools anywhere you go . . . that don't care really. But they'll think twice before they do it now. And that's why I say like Malcolm X, "Violence sometimes serves its purpose."

However, fighting between the Vice Lords and Cobras continued to flare up intermittently, and even during the time of my field work fights between groups of the two clubs still occurred.

After 1962 definite signs of stress in the Vice Lord organization began to show. During this time there were several feuds between various subgroups within the Vice Lord federation. Some of these feuds were between branches, while others were between individuals competing for the leadership of a particular branch. Following the imprisonment of many of the older boys who had been important leaders in the club's early days, the solidarity of the Vice Lord federation weakened even further. There was little communication between branches, and many branch leaders did not even know one another. Further, the original branch, the City Lords, became divided into what were called "sections." These sections were cliques which had developed into subbranches. Each section had a different name and set of officers. One section called the St. Louis Lords tried to gain even more autonomy from the City Lords by changing their name from Conservative Vice Lords to Mighty Vice Lords, and even went so far as to start their own female auxiliary known as the Supreme Queens. All girls connected with the club had previously been called Vice Ladies.

Sometime during 1963, the Imperial Chaplains completely broke up, and a short time later a new club, called the Roman Saints, was formed in a part of the Imperials' old neighborhood. It was not long before various branches of the Vice Lords became involved in gang fights with this new group. However, the fighting between the Vice Lords and the Roman Saints was never as intense as that between the Vice Lords and Cobras, although intermittent conflicts with the Roman Saints continued to the time of my field work.

In the summer of 1966 there was a new development in the Vice Lords' organization. This was brought about by several circumstances. First, the jail terms of many of the original leaders terminated. These individuals were no longer boys, but ranged in age from about 23 to 26. Rather than give up their gang membership, they decided to stay in the group. They also brought new members, other men their age, into the Vice Lords. Second, the Blackstone Rangers, a fighting club located on the South Side, began to receive newspaper publicity due to a gang war with the Devil's Disciples. In fact, one of Chicago's daily newspapers ran a week-long series on this group. In this series it was stated that the Blackstone Rangers were perhaps the toughest, best organized gang Chicago had seen for some time. In reaction to this series I heard comments from Vice Lords about how the group was falling apart; how they used to have an organization, but it was going downhill. Finally, after the riots which occurred on the West Side in the summer of 1966, the feelings of many Vice Lords turned away from Black Nationalism. I was told that some Black Nationalist groups had made promises to the Vice Lords that were not kept. At this time there was also an increase in hostile incidents between groups of Vice Lords and Roman Saints and Cobras. A meeting was called to discuss the future of the club. Although I was not present, I was told later that Bull, who was a member of a militant Black Nationalist organization, had spoken out against a resumption of gang fighting. He felt that all the clubs on the West Side should stop fighting among themselves and unite against the Whites. Others thought that the club's first responsibility was to protect its own members. I was told that, in answer to Bull, another Vice Lord said, "The Cobras may be my 'brothers,' but if one of them mother fuckers jump on me I'll bust a cap in his ass [shoot him]!" The overwhelming number of Vice Lords felt that the group should reorganize to protect themselves and their neighborhoods from hostile clubs, and to re-establish the reputation lost to the Blackstone Rangers. According to my informant, Bull might have been jumped on for his views if he had not left the meeting early.

The decision was made to reorganize the club, and the responsibility for working out the details was given to a group composed of representatives from each branch, along with the older individuals that had just been released from prison. The most important element in the new organizational scheme which resulted from the discussions of this group was the creation of an administrative body called the "board" to deal with matters affecting the entire Vice Lord Nation. Further, regular weekly meetings were instituted with representatives from all the subgroups present. Finally membership cards were printed with the Vice Lord's insignia—a top hat, cane, and white gloves. Every Lord in the Nation was required to pay an initial membership fee of 1 dollar, have his nickname written on the club's rolls, and carry his card with him at all times.

In the fall of 1968 I visited the Lords in their new business office on 16th Street, a few doors west of 16th and Lawndale. There had been numerous changes since I had done my first field work. The club was now legally incorporated, and had received a substantial grant from government sources to undertake self-help projects. The group had started a restaurant called "Teen Town," begun an employment service, and opened a recreation center named "House of Lords." They had entered into agreements with both the Cobras and the Roman Saints, and all three of the clubs had cooperated in community help projects. The Vice Lords were strongly involved in Black pride and Black consciousness programs. A staff of both Whites and Blacks was working in the Vice Lord office on legal problems faced by

The new Vice Lord restaurant on the corner of 16th and Lawndale.

members of the Lawndale community. In the short time I was there, however, it was impossible for me to get more than a few hints as to the basic changes the club had undergone. There were still various Vice Lord branches, but sections no longer functioned within Vice Lord City. Everyone I talked with, including friends who no

A group of Vice Lords outside their recreation center.

longer took part in any of the club's activities, said that gang fighting had completely stopped. If this is true, then it is clear to me that the Vice Lord social and cultural systems must have undergone basic and radical changes. The inflow of a large amount of money from government sources coupled with the complete termination of gang fighting must have had a profound impact on the group. Unfortunately, I was unable to go into any of this in the few hours of my visit. It will be fascinating to see what happens to the Vice Lords in the future.

In this chapter we have discussed the Vice Lords' origin and subsequent development. While this sketch is only an outline, most of the major developments in the club's growth have been highlighted. In the following chapters we shall turn from historical developments, and look more carefully into the club's social and cultural system as it existed at the time of my fieldwork in 1966. I will use the "ethnographic present" in my description, meaning that I will employ the present tense, even though the events occurred in the past, during the time I did the fieldwork.

Features of the Vice Lord
Social System

W HEN VICE LORDS DISCUSS THEIR CLUB, references are often made to particular features. Certain of these figured in the previous outline of Vice Lord development, and all are important to the discussions in later chapters. Here our concern is to introduce and briefly describe these features so that the arguments in later chapters can be followed.

Branches

The Vice Lord Nation is divided into "branches." Each branch has its own particular name, set of officers, and territory. At the time of my first period of field-work, Vice Lords said that the following branches existed—the Albany Lords, the California Lords, the 5th Avenue Lords, the Lake Street Lords, the Lexington Lords, the Madison Lords, the Maniac Lords, the City Lords (that is, those from Vice Lord City), and the War Lords. However, I cannot verify that all of these branches actually exist, for not every individual could name every branch, and leaders could not always be designated for the branches named. The Vice Lords who gave me information were from Vice Lord City, the Albany Lords, and the Monroe Lords. In addition I met Vice Lords from the Maniac Lords, the Sacramento Lords, and the War Lords. This indicates that the club is divided into at least these six branches.

Everyone I talked with agreed that the City Lords is the original branch; it is the largest and probably the most powerful subgroup in the Vice Lord Nation. The Vice Lord Social Center was located in Vice Lord City, the territory of the City Lords. Before it closed for lack of funds, the Center was a meeting place for all the Lords in the Nation. Vice Lords stated that each branch, while autonomous, gener-

ally acknowledges the seniority of the City Lords. Prior to the latest change in organization, the leaders of the City called the infrequent meetings of the entire Nation,
decided what was going to be discussed, and ran the actual meeting. The members
of the City were in charge of maintaining order. Although some branches may have
been feuding, no fighting was allowed during these meetings.

The number of branches is not constant—old branches break up, and new
ones are formed. One of the ways branches are formed is through alliance and subsequent absorption. The formation of the Monroe Lords provides a good example
of this process. A club known as the Ambassadors started fighting a club called the
Imperial Burpies. The Ambassadors lost fight after fight, and finally agreed to become a part of the Burpies. When the Vice Lords contacted the leaders of the Ambassadors and agreed to help them if the fight with the Burpies was renewed, the
Ambassadors withdrew from the Burpies, and the two groups again began fighting.
With the help of the Vice Lords, the Ambassadors won this war and broke up the
Burpies. The Ambassadors and the remnants of the Burpies became the Monroe
Lords.

In other instances branches are formed when groups of boys decide to start a
Vice Lord branch in their own neighborhood. After hanging with the Lords on
16th and Lawndale—the "capital" of Vice Lord City—and proving themselves to
be regular fellows, the leaders of the City Lords allow them to set up their own
branch and to use the Vice Lord name.

Toward the end of my field work I witnessed the formation of a branch by
this process. Some of the boys living in a neighborhood that was part of the North
Side ghetto were jumped on by a group of older boys who lived several blocks
away. The younger boys reacted to this in the standard ghetto way—they formed a
club for mutual protection. Some of these boys were friendly with a woman in the
neighborhood who offered them the use of her basement for their club meetings.
This woman was a good friend of several Vice Lords, and one afternoon they decided to visit her. She suggested to one of them that he talk to this group about
becoming a branch of the Vice Lords. When this individual showed the boys his
Vice Lord membership card and described how powerful the Lords were, they decided to try to become a part of the club. That weekend these boys sponsored a
dance, and several Vice Lords from the West Side came to help in case enemies of
the group might try to break it up. I was told that later the boys would be taken to
the West Side to meet other leaders of the Vice Lords, and after a short time,
would probably be accepted as Vice Lords by the leaders of the City.

Finally, new branches are formed as a result of the high rate of spatial mo-
bility found in the ghetto. As members of various branches move out of a neighborhood, they often start new branches in their new neighborhoods. Since they are already known as Vice Lords, it is not necessary for them to prove themselves further.

According to various Vice Lords, branches are often connected by ties of alliance which become activated during interbranch conflicts. These alliances are based
on individual friendships: Particular alliances often stem from the maintenance of
friendship ties between members who move away and join or found new branches,
and those who remain. When a conflict develops between two branches, others are
drawn in through the operation of ties based on friendship. An example is provided

by a feud between the Maypole and Monroe Lords. A Monroe Lord gives the following account of the early phases of this feud:

> This was one of them come-and-go fights. We strike and they strike. They were coming over in our neighborhood and jumping on the little boys and taking their money. Now we kept a strong neighborhood. We didn't do this, and we didn't allow it to go on. And the little kids looked up to us. They knew we were real bad, but they still thought we were nice.
>
> So one day some of the Maypole Lords came across Garfield Park and took some money from Jesse's little brother. Jesse, he was one of the heavy [important] Monroe Lords. We had to do something. We had told them not to come over robbing anybody. So we caught them in this little restaurant one night . . . unaware. And that's when the fighting broke out. We had quite a little humbug.

Fights between the Monroe and Maypole Lords continued, and other branches became involved. The Madison and California Lords supported the Monroe Lords, while the City Lords were allied with the Maypole branch. The following account by a member of the City Lords illustrates the principle of reciprocal friendship on which alliances between branches are based:

> The Maypole Lords, we dug them, but we didn't like the Monroe 'cause they was kind of funny—they was kind of bourgeois. They would give sets [parties] and stuff, and wouldn't let the City and Maypole know about it. We would find out afterwards. So why didn't they tell us? Then they'd go around talking about us. They said, "Well, we don't want them fools out here!" They didn't want Tankson and them from Maypole around 'cause they were stone fools. As far as I was concerned they were real mellow, but Monroe didn't dig them. And then we got the idea that Monroe was just using our name . . . to keep other people off them. And when Monroe started fighting the Maypole Lords, well quite naturally we going to come into it. Cave was out [of jail] then, and Cave more than likely would take the Maypole's side. Monroe didn't dig this. See, the Maypole, they was our boys. That stud Tankson, the president, he was a mellow stud. They were out of sight, and we dug them.

While branches may engage in feuds, they unite when threatened by an enemy club. The Monroe and the Maypole Lords united against the Racketeers even while their feud was in progress:

> Now while this [the feud between the Monroe and Maypole branches] was going on, the Racketeers was steady coming over. They were throwing gas bombs, and they had got pretty good at it. But we united with the Maypole Lords and trapped them over in Douglas Park . . . which they weren't expecting. They had done wrong, and they knew they had done wrong; before they knew it, we were on them! This was both us and the Maypole Lords. It was about two days after we had got the Maypole Lords in the restaurant. But the fight between us was still going on. We were still mad with them, and they were still mad because we had beat up a lot of them, and tore up their hangout.

In feuds between branches Vice Lords state that fighting should be limited to fists, although other weapons are sometimes used. In wars between clubs, in contrast, there are no limitations set on the legitimate use of weapons.

Sections

Within each branch there are various other kinds of subgroupings. The City Lords is the only group, however, that is divided into subgroups called sections. The sections that City Lords named are: the 15th Street Lords, the Ridgeway Lords, the St. Louis Lords, and the Trumbull Lords. At first glance these groups seem to be identical to branches. However, when asked about this, City Lords insist that sections are not the same as branches, but are subdivisions of one particular branch—the City Vice Lords. We shall look at sections in greater detail in the next chapter. Here all that need be noted is that (1) sections claim to control particular parts of Vice Lord City; (2) sections had a distinct set of offices before the recent reorganization, while after it they had only one office; and (3) the leaders of sections are considered more subordinant to the leaders of the City Lords than are those of other branches.

Age Groups

As stated in chapter 1, almost every branch of the Vice Lord Nation is divided into a set of subdivisions which Vice Lords call "Seniors," "Juniors," and "Midgets." Some branches even have "Pee Wee" Vice Lords. There is no cover term to refer to such groupings, but since age is an important basis for distinguishing between them, I have chosen to call them age groups.

In most branches each age group has its own set of officers. In the City Lords, however, this is not the case at the present time. Before the development of sections within the City Lords, each age group did have its own officers, but at the time of my field work such groups had no internal organization.

Membership in age groups varies between branches. In the City Lords the Midgets are usually 12 to 15, the Juniors are 16 to 17, and the Seniors are 18 and over. In the Monroe Lords the situation is quite different. Generally, the Midgets are boys 16 years of age and older who are small in size, the Seniors are boys 16 and older who are large, and the Juniors are all those under 16, regardless of size. However, individual choice is the most important consideration in age group membership. In the Monroe Lords an individual is usually free to join whatever age group he chooses as long as that group will accept him. If at a later time he wishes to change his age group affiliation, he is free to do so providing the members of the other group will accept him.

A comparison of age groupings among the Monroe and City Lords following the development of sections shows definite differences. In the Monroe Lords age divisions form distinct social groups, that is, they are internally structured. In contrast, at present these are only social categories in the City Lords. This is reflected in the way Vice Lords discuss events concerning the club with each other. In conversations I heard between individuals in the Monroe and Albany Lords, and between members of the City Lords who were talking about events that took place before the development of sections, particular people were often identified in terms of the age group to which they belonged, and events discussed in terms of age groups which had taken part in them. One of the older members of the City Lords who was talking about the "old days" provides an example.

> The roughest boys I ever met, they was between the ages of 13 and 15—Lil' Lord, Rough-head and them. They was the Midgets—the Midget Lords. And these were the baddest boys I ever went up against! What happened, they beat up one of the Senior Lords, a stud called Dough Belly. And Cave Man wouldn't even mess with the Midget Lords' cause they had so many guns. We didn't know where they got the guns from, but they used to bring them around and give them to us.

In contrast I never heard any of the City Lords allude to age groupings when discussing contemporary events. In these instances individuals were referred to in terms of their section membership.

The Vice Ladies

The Vice Ladies is the name of the female auxiliary connected with the Vice Lords. My information concerning the Vice Ladies comes from Vice Lords only, and, therefore, is incomplete. I was told there is a Vice Lady group attached to each branch. At one time there seem to have been Vice Ladies connected with certain sections of Vice Lord City, but this is not the case at the present time.

It is said that each Vice Lady group is independent of the Vice Lord branch to which it is connected. Vice Lady groups elect their own sets of officers, hold their own meetings, and make their own group decisions. There is no norm that Vice Lords should monopolize sexual rights in Vice Ladies—many Vice Ladies are said to go with Cobras, and some Vice Lords say their girlfriends are Cobraettes, the Cobra female auxiliary. On the other hand, this independence is not always complete. In Vice Lord City the girl who goes with the president of the City Lords is generally considered to be the head of the City Vice Ladies. There is often strong hostility between Vice Ladies and Vice Lords, and in several instances this has taken the form of actual fighting.

> Every once in a while we used to fight with the Vice Ladies. They was boss humbuggers, Jack! [Boss—very good, humbuggers—fighters.] I remember one night we had a fight with them and they got us. Jesse was out there at the time— Jesse Clayborn. Jesse's a stone fool! He was out there rolling a tire—playing with this broad Rose. I don't know what was wrong with her. She was in the Vice Ladies, and she had a quick temper. She high at the time anyway. So they was rolling a tire back and forth. Jesse rolled the tire, and Rose missed catching it, and it knocked her down. Now Rose was high and crazy, and Jesse crazy too. Rose got mad. She jumped up and pulled out a knife . . . long knife, Jack! And Jesse got a stick. You know, he going to bust her in the head with that stick! So all the girls jumped up. They not going to go for this. One of them said, "Look at him! Got a big stick after that girl!" Jesse said, "She got a knife! If she try to cut me with that knife, I'll bust her in the head with this stick!"

So all the Vice Ladies started picking up bricks and carrying on. They going to help Rose. By then I had grabbed Rose around the waist. I was holding her, and Shotgun was holding her. Killer, he had on a pair of leather gloves, so he took the knife out of her hand.

But Rose said, "That don't mean shit! That ain't nothing!" and Jesse and her started going from the cuff. They was actually out there boxing. So Rose, she was so tore up [high] that she accidentally hit another one of the fellows named Lonzo, and he hit her back. That really got the Vice Ladies shook up. So when he hit Rose, this girl Ella Mae, she hit Lonzo with a stick . . . yeah, in the head with a stick. So Lonzo picked up a brick. He going to hit the broad with a brick. And everybody started picking up weapons off the ground—anything they could lay their hands on. Half the fellows wanted to go on and dust the girls, but the other half were going with them, and quite naturally they didn't. So while the fellows were arguing among themselves about what they should do, well, the girls were popping us in the head with sticks and bottles and bricks. I got hit myself . . . right in the eye. Rose hit me. They really messed us up that night.

Offices

Formal offices are found in various branches, age groups, and sections of the Vice Lord Nation. Before the latest reorganization, there were seven named offices, although all were not found in every subgroup. These offices are: president, vice-president, secretary-treasurer, supreme war counselor, war counselor, gunkeeper, and sergeant-at-arms. The information I was given concerning these offices can be summarized in the following manner:

1. The president conducts meetings, in some cases makes the decision whether or not to fight another group, and is responsible for leading successful raids. He symbolizes the group's power, and in feuding and warfare his injury is the prime objective of enemy force.

2. The vice-president is the president's assistant. He has few formally recognized duties. When the president has been arrested, or otherwise cannot or will not fulfill his duties, the vice-president succeeds to the office of president.

3. The war counselor is the president's main assistant when the group is involved in fighting. He is specifically charged with the responsibility of deciding whether or not to begin a fight in a confrontation between two rival groups. No one is supposed to begin fighting until the war counselor throws the first punch, or, as the case may be, fires the first shot. In the Albany Midgets there are three war counselors: a supreme war counselor and two regular war counselors. The war counselors, along with the president, form a war council which decides whether or not the group will fight when one of its members has been attacked by individuals outside the group. All decisions have to be approved by a majority of the council. If a decision to fight is made, the supreme war counselor organizes and leads the raid. Much of the fighting that informants discussed followed accidental encounters between enemy cliques, and in such cases war counselors have no institutionalized responsibilities.

Cliques

Branches and sections are subdivided into a set of what I call cliques that are basic units in the Vice Lord social system. In the jargon of the streets a group of individuals in a clique are referred to as "running partners." These groups are important in warfare, political power struggles, and social activities. Membership in cliques sometimes crosscuts age groups, but never sections or branches. Within cliques, in contrast to branches, sections, and in some instances, age groups, leadership in not institutionalized into a set of formally recognized offices. For example, in one clique in the City Lords before the development of sections, one of the leaders was secretary-treasurer of the Seniors, while another was president of the Juniors. Within the clique itself, neither was considered to outrank the other.

Many cliques have their own name and status in a ranked hierarchy. In Vice Lord City a few years ago the "Magnificent Seven" was the most powerful. Another powerful group was known as the "Rat Pack." At present in the Sacramento Lords the most important of these groups is called the "Gallant Men."

Cliques play a crucial role in power struggles within the branch organization. According to Vice Lords, cliques sometimes fight one another in support of rival leaders vying for positions of power within the branch. The following story was told about a fight between the Rat Pack and the Magnificent Seven:

> What happened was whenever one of these civic groups give a dance they would invite Cave Man, and he would bring a couple of the fellows, he would get some of these new fellows that had just got in the club. So I told Cave Man, I said, "Cave, why don't you get a couple of older fellows and take them around?" And the YMCA was having some of the fellows be field assistants and consultants, and Cave Man was picking out the guys, but he was picking out the wrong fellows. So I told him about it . . . at the club meeting. I said, "I'm about to give it up . . . seeing how you all running everything. I'm tired of this! I got so many fellows with me, and Cool Fool got so many with him, we could start something of our own." I said, "Cave, you just one man, and there's a whole lot of us. We really are the backbone of the club." So those dudes in the Magnificant Seven, Cave and them, they got mad.
>
> Now when I first got in the club, I was real small dude, but I had put on a little weight, and I had got tall. The next day we was all in the pool room over on Roosevelt. So a dude called Fresh-up Freddie, he was in the Magnificent Seven, he said, "Just because you've got big, I bet you believe you can whup me." I said, "I didn't say nothing like that, but I . . ." He said, "Come outside!" So we went outside and we started boxing. He couldn't touch me, so I said, "I quit," and I dropped my guard. That mother fucker, he hit me in the nose, hit me in the mouth, and my mouth started bleeding.
>
> Now Cool Fool had my jive [gun]. I said, "Fool, gimme my jive!" and Fool, he gave me my gun. I said to Fresh-up, "I ought to shoot you!"
>
> Now Fresh-up got the intention of snatching the gun. He done snatched three or four guns out of different fellows hands, and he started walking at me. He said, "Shoot me if you want to. I don't believe you going to shoot me." I knew what he's going to do when he got close, he going to grab the gun. I didn't want to kill him so I shot him in his arm. I had to shoot him. You see, if I hadn't done it, he would of took my gun away from me. So I went straight home. Cool

Fool and the rest of our fellows, they stayed around the pool hall. There was a boss humbug.

New Organization

Under the new organization, each branch remains fairly autonomous. However, there is an executive body of 8 members that deals with problems affecting the club as a whole. This group, known as the "board," is made up of representatives from each major branch along with some of the older members from various branches. The board is headed by a president chosen from among its members. A council of about 20 members from various branches backs up the board. If a member of the board is arrested, it is planned that his replacement will be chosen from this group.

The board is supposed to function as an advisory rather than a decision-making group. As we have seen, under the old organization the president or war council of a particular branch decided whether the group would fight. In matters pertaining to a war involving all the branches, in theory the president of the City Lords had this power. Under the new organization, however, it is the group as a whole which carries the responsibility for making such a decision. The board would bring the problem to the group during a weekly meeting, and the group would decide what course of action to take. Vice Lords give a definite reason for making the group rather than the president responsible for such decisions.

> We noticed that it put a lot of pressure up on one guy to make a decision alone. Like, for instance, just think what would happen if we having trouble from some guys—the Cobras or the Roman Saints—and Cave stood up and said, "Well, we fight them." The minute he says this, then this means he gave the order to start it. But when you put it to a board, the board don't say, "Well, we fight them." The board ask the group, "What is your decision about this?" and they make their own decision. The board say, "Well, we with the fellows." Then no one guy had made no decision. See what I mean, the group has made the decision, and ain't no one man have the responsibility. In other words, this is the way to eliminate the problem of the law. In the past when somebody got killed or hurt they could come and pick up one man, and actually charge him with the murder 'cause he gave the order. This way they just have to come and get the group, and they can't do that. So they just have to pin point the man—the one who actually pulled the trigger. But this is almost impossible to do.

Within Vice Lord City the sections were abolished as formal semi-independent subdivisions. Nevertheless, the individuals who had formed sections were to choose leaders, called "lieutenants," to be responsible in gang wars for mobilizing their group, defending a particular part of Vice Lord City, and leading their group in attacks on the enemy.

Finally, three individuals were chosen to comprise what is called the "death squad." If a Vice Lord is attacked by another club, and the group as a whole does not decide to go to war, then a member of the death squad is given the responsibility for organizing and leading a small retaliatory raid.

Membership

It is extremely difficult, if not impossible, to determine the size of the Vice Lord Nation. The leaders themselves do not have a really accurate idea of how many members the club has. I received estimates from various individuals ranging from 600 to 3000. One way to get a figure would be to do a census of each branch. However, the size of their group is one of the things branch members are most reticent to talk about, and I was only able to do a census on the section of the City Lords called the 15th Street Vice Lords. In any case a census of all the branches would still fail to produce a completely accurate figure, for it is not always clear in what sense particular individuals are members of the club. For instance, a person may get a job, start supporting a family, and cease to take part in most Vice Lord activities. Occasionally, however, he may come out on the corner, drink wine, and shoot craps with other Vice Lords. While he is on the corner, he acts like and is treated by others as a Vice Lord. It then becomes problematical whether one would wish to count this particular person as a part of the club. A possible solution would be to count as members those individuals who are defined by others as Vice Lords. In many cases, however, there is real disagreement concerning whether a particular person is actually a member. Further, an individual himself may claim to be a part of the group in one instance, but deny he is a member at other times. Given the changes in organization, theoretically it should be possible to obtain a fairly accurate figure of the group's size since everyone in the club is supposed to have a membership card and his name placed on the club rolls. In actuality I found that certain individuals did not have membership cards, did not have their names on the rolls, but were still considered by some to belong to the club in certain situations. When I asked Vice Lords about these inconsistencies, the matter was shrugged off as essentially unimportant.

Ignoring this problem for the moment, one can make a very rough approximation of the Vice Lords' size, although I doubt whether in the final analysis it is even a meaningful undertaking. The 15th Street Lords have at the least thirty members. If we assume this to be typical of the other sections in Vice Lord City, then the City Lords probably number at least 150. Counting the other branches, the total number of Vice Lords may fall somewhere between the figures of 600 and 3000 given by the Vice Lords.

According to all accounts, the Vice Lords have no standard initiation for new members. Initiation varies both among the different subgroups in the club, and among the various individuals involved. In some cases a boy simply moves into a neighborhood which has a Vice Lord group and hangs with members of the club. He participates in certain activities with them, "runs" with them on the streets, and gradually takes part in more and more of their activities until finally he is considered a member.

Sometimes a boy will commit some act that gives him prestige in the eyes of club members and he will be asked to join. An example of this is a boy called Mad Dog. Mad Dog moved into Vice Lord City. His first day in the neighborhood he was challenged by two younger brothers of one of the club's "heavy" members. In

Herzel School located on 15th Street. In the past Vice Lords often used the school grounds at Herzel for meetings.

the fight that followed he not only "whupped" the two younger brothers, but the older brother as well. He was then invited to join the group. First, however, he was required to box with Cave Man, at that time the president of the City Lords. Following this, Cave Man and Mad Dog stood back to back and fought off other members of the club who came at them from all sides in what is called a free-for-all. Mad Dog fought until his jaw was dislocated. Since he had won the respect of the club members, he was considered a full-fledged member.

In most cases, however, becoming fully accepted as a member occurs over a period of time. The president of the 15th Street Lords gives the following account of how an individual becomes a member of his particular group:

> Like you a new member, and you join the 15th Street Lords. Now you haven't got no name or nothing, and we haven't exactly got one right off hand so we'll look at the chart. See, we have a chart of all the nicknames—Emp, Roughhead, Bat Masterson, Windy, Chico, Pico, Rico. Then I asks the group, "Who want this man to be named after him?" And one of the fellows raise their hand and say, "He can be named after me." So I'll say, "Your name is little Tico, and this Big Tico." Now Big Tico supposed to make sure you do everything right. He show you how to do it . . . take you around, introduce you to the neighborhood. He let you see the neighborhood, how it is, how we got it arranged and everything. But all the while Big Tico doing this he not going to take you to the regular hideout 'till about three weeks after you joined. And all the three weeks you being watched—to see where you go; when you leave the house; what neighborhood you go in; who you be walking with and what time of the day. We checking you out in other words. We don't know, you might be a Cobra.

Territory

Vice Lords call the space they control "territory." It is that part of Chicago in which there is little chance that a Vice Lord will be attacked by an enemy group, but a significantly larger chance that a member of an enemy club will be attacked by a group of Vice Lords. Any Vice Lord, regardless of clique, section, age group, or branch can go into any part of the territory controlled by the Vice Lord Nation and he will not be attacked by a Vice Lord group. For example, if a member of the City Lords has a girlfriend who lives in the territory of the Albany Lords, he knows that he will not be jumped on by a group of Albany Lords when he visits her. If a member of the Albany Lords also goes with this girl, then there may be a fight between the two concerning the girl. However, this should be a "man-to-man" fight, and other Albany Lords should not take an active part. If other Albany Lords did take part in such a fight, with the result that a City Lord was beaten by a group of Albany Lords, this would constitute a repudiation of the Albany Lords' membership in the Vice Lord Nation. It would signal that the Albany Lords now considered themselves to be separate from, and an enemy of, the rest of the Vice Lords.

Branch territory is not contiguous. Branches are spatially separated from one another both by territory of enemy clubs and by segments of the ghetto that are not controlled by any club. Within Vice Lord City particular sections are also linked to territory. Section territories, unlike branch territories, are in some cases contiguous. Not all of Vice Lord City, however, is claimed by particular sections. The heart of the City—the corner of 16th and Lawndale—is the meeting place and hangout for all the members of the City Lords, and is not a part of any section. There are other parts of Vice Lord City which are of no particular significance, but are also, like the corner of 16th and Lawndale, not thought to belong to any section. The outline map below shows both territorial divisions of Vice Lord City and boundaries with enemy clubs. The map below shows Vice Lord City as forming a distinct, bounded territorial unit, but this picture is somewhat misleading. Vice Lord territory is that part of Chicago where Vice Lords (but not members of other clubs) are relatively free from attack. The map shows the territory claimed by the Vice Lords, but Vice Lords are not equally free from attack in all portions of that territory. As one approaches the boundaries of other clubs, the chance that a Vice Lord will be attacked by an enemy group increases. At an actual boundary with an enemy club there is roughly an equal chance that a Vice Lord will be jumped on as there is that a member of the enemy club will be jumped on. If the boundary is crossed, then the chance that a Vice Lord will be jumped on is greater than the chance that members of the enemy club will be jumped on by Vice Lords.

I first began to understand how Vice Lords think about territory in listening to a discussion concerning the Central Park—a movie house located on Central Park and Roosevelt Road (12th Street). A number of 15th Street Lords were discussing whether to go to the show. In the discussion it was mentioned that the Vice Lords used to "have" the Central Park show, but that it now "belonged" to the Roman Saints. This was answered by, "Yeah man, we owned that Central Park show!

Looking south on Pulaski, the boundary between Vice Lord City and K-Town.

The northwest corner of 16th and Lawndale.

The southwest corner of 16th and Lawndale.

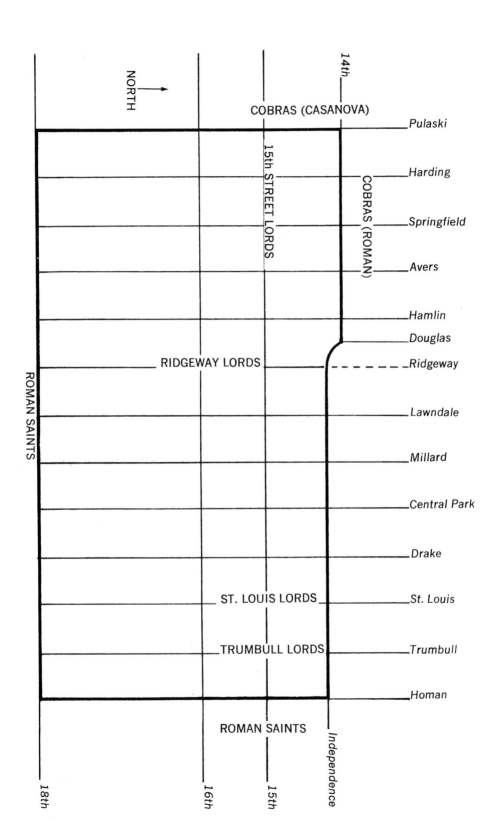

Couldn't none of them Roman Saints come. They was afraid, Jack! They knew we'd whup their ass!" The discussion concluded with the admission that Vice Lords had lost the Central Park show to the Roman Saints, and unless it was worth risking a gang fight, it would be better not to go to the show in a group. When I matched this with how particular Vice Lords had explained the concept of territory to me, the way Vice Lords think about territory became clear:

> The 15th Street Lords' territory is from 15th and Ridgeway all the way to Pulaski. This is our territory 'cause can't nobody come through—no off-brand clubs.

> The territory of the 15th Street Lords is from 15th and Ridgeway to 15th and Pulaski. We have mostly all of it up tight. This means that no other groups can come down in our hood and start nothing. If we didn't have it up tight we'd have to try and get it up tight—get it organized. If we didn't have it up tight, then dudes could come by and jump on us and the other people in the neighborhood.

This discussion of territory shows how Vice Lords distinguish their own territory from that of enemy clubs; but what distinguishes between the territory of different sections? To illustrate an important point, I will digress a bit and include several interviews in which I was trying to find out how various section territories are distinguished. In working with informants the most difficult task is to formulate the right questions. However, in order to be able to ask the right questions, one has to have a fairly accurate idea of what the right answer might be. In these particular sessions, my idea of what the right answer might be was so inaccurate that it kept me from perceiving the significance of what I was told.

R. L. K.: What's the territory of the Ridgeway Lords?
Duck: Ridgeway, all the way from 18th to Independence.
R. L. K.: Where do most of the Ridgeway Lords hang out?
Duck: On 16th Street. There be very few on Ridgeway.
R. L. K.: If they all hang out on 16th Street, why aren't they considered 16th Street Lords?
Duck: 16th Street just a hangout for everybody.
R. L. K.: When you say that's the territory of the Ridgeway Lords, what do you mean? What does it mean that you have that territory?
Duck: Everybody got their little section where they hang out at. It's just different street names. They just go by street names, that's all.
R. L. K.: Well, is it because they live on that street, or is it because they hang out on that street?
Duck: They hang out on that street, and most of them live on the street, but you don't have to live on the street.
R. L. K.: O.K., suppose you live on Ridgeway, and you're in the Ridgeway Lords, and you move away; does that change your membership, or can you still belong?
Duck: You can still belong.
R. L. K.: But if you start hanging around with the group where you live now will that change your membership?
Duck: Not exactly. I keep telling you we all the same. You can belong to one group, but you can hang out wherever you want.

I had assumed (almost unconsciously) that section territory was differentiated in terms of rights, and it was this idea that directed my questioning. However, after this interview I was obviously no closer to understanding the basis for section territorial distinctions. I failed to realize that my questions were based on an incorrect assumption about what the right answers might be, and in the next interview I worked from the same direction. Therefore, I not only missed an important clue but also thought I found the basis for the distinction which was, in fact, not the case at all.

R. L. K.:   As a member of the Ridgeway Lords, what is the difference between my territory and your territory?

Earl: They trying to keep the Roman Saints from falling down on us, and we trying to keep the Cobras from falling down on them. We got two different groups coming from two different ways. From the east its the Roman Saints, and from the west its the Cobras. We trying to hold the Cobras back far as we can so they won't get closer to 16th and Lawndale, 'cause 15th Street is the back door to the City.

R. L. K.:   What I'm trying to get at is the difference having a particular territory means for individuals in different groups. Now I don't know if this is the case, but are there certain things that Ridgeway Lords can do in their territory that they can't do in your territory.

Earl: You right there. Like some of the 15th Street Lords might go over there— they ain't got no business jumping on no one over there, and they ain't got no business coming over to our hood and jumping on somebody.

The first answer should have given me a clue as to how Vice Lords distinguish between section territories, but because I assumed there must be differences in rights, I failed to see its significance. When I asked Earl to give me an answer in terms of rights, he did. This simply led me further along a blind alley. It was not until the interview with Big Otis that I finally understood the basis for territorial distinctions between sections. I started this interview with the same assumption. Fortunately, Goliath, one of my best informants, closest friends, and roommate for the summer, was present. He saw at once what I was trying to find out, and why I was getting nowhere. Goliath provided the right questions to ask as well as the right answer.

Goliath: What advantages do you have in your own territory?

Big Otis: We know all the gangways and rooftops, and we know just about everybody in the streets.

Goliath: Do you use your territory also like a meeting place? Like for instance all the fellows get together to go someplace and take care of business [get together for a raid], could you all meet in this same area, could you get together right away, like could you contact everybody?

Big Otis: Yeah, you know where to find them at. You know where all the places they be at.

Goliath: In other words, you wouldn't have to worry about the Cobras coming down and whupping you in your territory.

Big Otis: No, we know it before they get down there.

R. L. K.:   How is this different from the territory of the Ridgeway Lords?

Big Otis: It's no different.

R. L. K.:   Why isn't the territory of the Ridgeway Lords your territory? What makes it different?

Goliath: See, everybody in one box, like for instance Roach and them, they be on
             15th Street, so they make sure don't nobody come down Ridgeway that we
             don't know. This way you block off the whole area, and there always be
             somebody around. If you can't handle it, then you get help.
Big Otis: Yeah, if the Cobras coming from one end and the Saints coming from
             another its our job on 15th Street to stop the Cobras.

It is apparent that the distinction between section territories is based on differential responsibility rather than differential rights. Sections have the responsibility of
protecting particular parts of Vice Lord City from enemy attacks. A section's territory,
therefore, is that particular part of Vice Lord City for which it is responsible in case
of enemy attack. In order to fulfill this responsibility, section members must have a
good knowledge of how their territory is laid out—where gangways lead, how to
gain access to rooftops, what alleys are dead ends, and so forth. It is advantageous,
if not necessary to have such knowledge when section members must actually defend
their territory against enemy raids.

Our outline of the Vice Lords social system poses a particular problem. I
have described a set of groups and positions within the club that are significant to
Vice Lords, but in what sense do these form a system? In the following two chapters I shall attempt to answer this question.

3

The Social System—Groups

OUR PROBLEM IN THIS CHAPTER is to demonstrate how Vice Lord social behavior constitutes a system. A social system has been previously defined as the pattern of social interaction actualized in the ongoing process of interactive behavior. (Geertz 1957:33–34). In attempting to describe the pattern in Vice Lord social behavior we shall identify forms which emerge in social interaction and principles on which social behavior is based.

In observing Vice Lords in action over a period of time one finds a recurring series of situations in which behavior follows a particular pattern. Situations like this are generally called "social contexts" by anthropologists, but could just as well be called "happenings"—to borrow a particularly apt term from the hipster. Vice Lords themselves recognize certain social contexts, or happenings, as being distinct, and refer to them in certain ways. Some are given particular names, for example, "gangbangs," "sets," and "meetings." Others are designated by the kinds of activities that occur within them, such as: "pulling jive," "shooting craps," "hustling," and "wolf packing."

If we look at the behavior that takes place within social contexts, certain patterns emerge. One kind of pattern takes the form of what can be called "social roles." Social roles are both specific social identities and the particular kinds of behavior considered proper between individuals who assume these identities.

Another kind of pattern which emerges from interaction taking place within social contexts relates to social groups. In the last chapter we outlined the ways Vice Lords talk about various social groupings within their club, and we found that individuals are simultaneously members of a series of groups. But what gives these groups meaning? When, for example, is an individual's branch, as opposed to his age group, affiliation of significance? The answer is that Vice Lord social groups have meaning in terms of particular social contexts, for it is through interactive behavior which occurs within social contexts that social groups are given substance. Part of the pattern in the Vice Lord system is that similar kinds of social contexts give form to similar kinds of social groupings. In other words, we can find regularities in the particular social groups that emerge from the interaction taking place within particular social contexts.

We have identified three aspects of the pattern of Vice Lord social interaction: (1) There are recurring sets of behavior that are recognized by Vice Lords as forming distinct social contexts or "happenings"; (2) particular social roles systematically emerge from the interaction that takes place within these happenings; and (3) this interaction systematically gives form to particular social groups. In this chapter we are primarily concerned with social groups, while in the following chapter we shall focus on social roles.

In looking at the relationship between social contexts and social groups there are several observations that stand out. We find in some instances a direct correspondence between a particular social context and the group affiliation that is significant within that context. For other contexts there is a limited range of significant group affiliations—that is, certain social contexts limit the range of possible group affiliations that can be of significance to individuals acting in those contexts. Within this range the actual activation of any potential group affiliation is a function of choice. Nevertheless, it is possible to find regularities in such choices, and, therefore, principles can be isolated which specify what group will actually emerge in any given instance.

We shall be dealing mainly with data from the City Lords in our discussion of patterns in social interaction since most of my research was with this particular branch. However, I did gather some information on other branches which will also be brought into the discussion.

The Gangbang

The social context of a "gangbang" (gang fight) is considered by Vice Lords to be one of the most important social happenings in street life. How individuals behave in gangbangs is a constant topic of conversations, and is a crucial determinant of status and prestige. In a later chapter we shall look at the gangbang as a cultural scene, and consider the norms and values which are important to it. Here we are concerned with the relationship between gangbangs and the activation of group affiliations.

Among the City Lords we find three kinds of group affiliations that are activated in gangbangs—membership in a section; membership in the branch; and membership in the Vice Lord Nation. Clique and age-group affiliation are never meaningful in this context. In other branches that do not have sections, age group, as well as branch and Nation, affiliation can be significant.

What principles underlie the choice of one of the possible group affiliations in a gangbang rather than another? To answer this we first have to distinguish between variations in the range of situations Vice Lords call gangbangs, for this variation is related to the principles which generate choices of group affiliation. Gangbangs can occur in several ways. A collection of Vice Lords may accidentally encounter several members of an enemy club at a party, a dance, or a movie, and a gang fight results. In explaining gangbangs a Vice Lord gave the following account of this kind of gang fight.

> There are these accidental fights. Say you walking down the street with some of the fellows and you meet the Cobras. You're not really looking for them, but when you run up on them you go down [fight]. Or say, for instance, we going to a set [party] and it's out of our neighborhood. We really not looking for no fight, but we ready. So the Cobras decide to come too. You all might get along 'til just about time the party's over, and then boom—everything goes down.

Gangbangs also result when Vice Lords either raid an enemy club, or when an enemy club raids them. In the first instance Vice Lords mobilize for attack, and the ensuing gangbang materializes as a Vice Lord raid on enemy territory. In the second instance Vice Lords mobilize for defense, and, in the resulting gangbang, defend against raiders from an enemy club. Gangbangs which do not result from accidental encounters usually stem from instances where one or two members of a club are jumped on by a large number of individuals from another club. If Vice Lords are jumped on by members of another club, various Vice Lord groups often mobilize for attack, while if a group of Vice Lords jump on members of another club, the Vice Lords will usually gather for purposes of defense. A Vice Lord explained this to me in the following way:

> If the Cobras come down and hurt one of the fellows and the president say "fall," we got to fall. When the president say "fall" that means that all the fellows supposed to get together and go down there [to the Cobra's territory]. Just say we going to fall tomorrow. The president and the vice-president get together, they talk, they say we going to fall at a certain time, and to meet at a certain place. When everybody meet, we all split up and go different ways. But we don't arrange to meet another club at a certain time or nothing like that.
> If the Cobras coming down in our hood, we be prepared for them. Like if we jumped on a Cobra and he hurt, this is what he going to do. He going to go down and tell his fellows. He going to say, "The Vice Lords jumped on me!" This is what they going to do. They done get mad and all riled up. They going to say, "We going down there on the Vice Lords!" When they come, we prepared. They come down 15th or maybe 14th. What we do, we lay back . . . maybe in just a couple of gangways, and when they fall out, we fall out on them.

Gangbangs can also result from fights between an individual Vice Lord and a member of another club. If the Vice Lord wins such a fight, the Vice Lords may be attacked by the other club, while if he loses, there may be a decision by a Vice Lord group to retaliate against the other club.

We have made the following distinctions in the situations that Vice Lords call gangbangs—gang fights that result from accidental encounters between Vice Lords and members of an enemy club, gang fights in which Vice Lords defend their territory against an enemy raid, and gang fights in which Vice Lords raid the territory of an enemy club. When we look at these distinctions in terms of group affiliations, it is possible to isolate the principles which generate the kind of group affiliation that will emerge as meaningful in any given gangbang context.

Accidental Encounters

In instances where gangbangs result from accidental encounters between Vice Lords and members of an enemy club we find the following principle determines which group affiliation will be significant: if the Vice Lords involved in the gangbang are members of the same section, then it is section membership that will be significant; if the Vice Lords are members of different sections, but the same branch, then it is branch membership that will be significant; and if the Vice Lords are members of different branches, it is club membership that will be significant. In branches that do not have sections, the principle works in a similar manner except that age groups replace sections as the narrowest group that can take on significance.

Vice Lords Defend

My information for gangbangs in which Vice Lords are defenders is limited to the City Lords. For the City, there are two kinds of groups which are mobilized for purposes of defense—sections, and the branch. Before proceeding further it is necessary to review the way Vice Lords think about territory, for territoriality is crucially related to ways group affiliations are given meaning. As we recall, the territory of the Vice Lord Nation is comprised of the noncontiguous territories of each branch. Vice Lord territory is that part of Chicago in which there is little chance that a Vice Lord will be attacked by an enemy group, but a significantly larger chance that a member of an enemy club will be attacked by a group of Vice Lords. Within Vice Lord City particular sections are linked to particular territories. "Section territory" is that part of Vice Lord City that sections are responsible for defending in case of enemy raids. Now let us return to the problem at hand.

In some cases an enemy attack is aimed at the territory of a particular section. In instances like this, section membership becomes meaningful. For example, late one night I came to the corner of 15th and Hamlin with Tex, the president of the 15th Street Lords. We had been standing there for about five minutes when Bat Man walked up and told us that there had been a fight earlier that evening between Shotgun and Excell. Excell was in the Roman Cobras, while Shotgun was one of the important members of the 15th Street Lords. Shotgun had won the fight, and it was felt that the Cobras might decide to "fall," that is, make a raid. Tex immediately started to organize for the defense of the territory. Bat Man was given instructions to find other 15th Street Lords who lived outside the territory and meet at a particular place at a certain time. Tex then went around the 15th Street Lords' territory collecting members of the section and placing them in strategic positions. Although the raid never materialized, a certain group of Vice Lords had been mobilized in terms of their responsibility to defend a particular segment of Vice Lord City. It was section membership that was significant in this instance.

There are other instances where Vice Lords feel an enemy raid is aimed at penetrating to the heart of Vice Lord City—the corner of 16th and Lawndale. In cases like this, both section and branch membership become significant. I observed a situation in which it was thought the Roman Saints were planning to attack 16th and Lawndale. Both the St. Louis Lords and the Trumbull Lords were mobilized for the defense of their territory since it was suspected that the Saints would come through that segment of Vice Lord City in order to get to 16th and Lawndale. (See map on page 24.) Thus certain members of the City Lords were mobilized in terms of their section membership for the defense of their territory. However, the rest of the City Vice Lords who gathered at 16th and Lawndale were organized for the defense of the corner by the leader of the branch. For these Vice Lords branch membership was significant.

The significance of group affiliation in cases where Vice Lords are defenders is based on differential responsibility for the defense of the branch. The group affiliation that will actually be significant depends on assessments of the enemy's aims. If it is believed that an enemy club plans to attack the territory of a particular section, then for those Vice Lords who have potential membership in that section, this membership is activated. If, however, it is believed that an enemy club plans an attack on the branch, for example, the corner of 16th and Lawndale, then section membership is activated for some, while branch membership is activated for others. The actual section membership that becomes activated depends on what enemy club is believed to be planning an attack, and from what direction it is thought the attack will come.

Vice Lords Attack

When a Vice Lord is beaten up by members of another club, certain Vice Lord subgroups are mobilized for retaliatory raids. In some instances sections form the raiding parties, while at other times branches, and even the entire Vice Lord Nation, may be mobilized for retaliation against an enemy club. This presents us with a set of problems. First, how can we account for instances in which Vice Lords actually retaliate when a member is jumped on by an enemy club, in contrast to instances when there is no retaliation? Then, looking only at the cases in which there is retaliation, how can we explain differences in the kinds of groups which function as raiding parties?

Although Vice Lords state that when a member is jumped on there should be retaliation, most admit that this does not always happen. Actually, retaliation depends on a variety of factors. If there has been a series of incidents (such as arguments and individual fights) between Vice Lords and members of another club, retaliation is likely. Competition for leadership within Vice Lord subgroups also affects the probability of retaliation. Strong competition for leadership increases the probability of retaliation, while lack of competition decreases it. Vice Lords feel that a rep as a brave warrior is a necessary qualification for occupying leadership positions, and thus the rep of competitors is highly valued political capital. If a competitor fails to call for retaliation when a member of the group is jumped on by an enemy club, his rival can accuse him of lacking "heart" (that is, roughly, bravery). Such an accusation can seriously weaken an individual's rep, and place him at a disadvantage vis-à-vis his rival. Therefore, leadership competition makes it politically expedient for contestants to uphold the norm of group retaliation for wrongs committed by an enemy club against its members. The result is that, other things equal, the probability of retaliation is higher when leadership is contested than when leaders are secure in their positions. A third factor affecting the incidence of retaliation is the status of the person who was jumped on. If the person is of low status—if he is neither a leader nor an important follower of a leader—then often some excuse will be given for not retaliating. In contrast, if the person is a highly respected leader, or an influential member of a particular Vice Lord subgroup, then retaliation is likely.

The status of the Vice Lord beaten up by an enemy club is also the crucial factor in determining which subgroup will be mobilized for retaliation. If the person jumped on is an influential leader in a section or strongly allied with an important section leader, but is not allied with any of the important branch or Nation leaders, then the group that may be mobilized for retaliation would be the section; if he has high status in a branch, but not the Nation, then the branch may be mobilized; and finally, if he is considered one of the "top Lords" in the Nation, then the entire Vice Lord Nation may be mobilized for the purpose of retaliation. There have been a few times when the entire Nation gathered for carrying out attacks. One such incident was a gang fight between the Vice Lords and the Imperial Chaplains (also known as the Commanches). I collected several different accounts of this fight—one is included in Chapter 6. It is striking that in all the accounts it is stated that the Vice Lords decided to attack the Imperials only after several of the most important Lords in the Nation had been jumped on by the Imperials. The following account provides a good example of how the status of the Vice Lord jumped on is crucially related to the kind of Vice Lord subgroup mobilized for retaliation. In reading this account it should be recalled that Cave Man is alleged to be the founder of the Vice Lords, and has always been the most influential person in the entire Nation. Even when he was not the actual president of the Nation he was the leader with the most *de facto* power.

It was about seven o'clock on Saturday when I came to 16th Street, and there was about forty or fifty boys on the corner. They were hollering and shouting and carrying on, Jack! So I asked them what was happening. They said that Cave Man, Tree Top, and a couple a more of the top Lords had went into the Imperials' neighborhood, and Cave had got hit across the eye with a stick. And someone started hollering, "You go over on Maypole! You get those fellows over on Maypole! You go out South, get the fellows out South! You go up to Albany and Monroe, and get those fellows! We'll meet back here at 16th and Lawndale in an hour and a half!" So I went home to get my shotgun.

We really messed them up that night, Jack! I cut three of them myself. What happened, I walked across the street and before I know, I got down [to get down is to do something really well]. It was Ghengis Khan, Big James, and Big House Willy. The first one ran into me . . . and I cut him. It was Big James. Ghengis Khan ran into me, and I cut him. Willy seen the knife, and he ran across the street.

We have discussed two aspects of gang fights in which Vice Lords attack an enemy club. First, we looked at the problem of instances in which Vice Lord groups retaliate against an enemy club, in contrast to instances in which there is no retaliation. We found that there are several factors that affect the probability of retaliation. If there have been a number of incidents between Vice Lords and an enemy club—such as arguments and fights between individuals—then the probability increases that the Vice Lords will retaliate when one of their members is beaten up by an enemy group. If there is strong competition for the leadership of a Vice Lord subgroup, the chance also increases that Vice Lords will retaliate when a Vice Lord is jumped on. Finally, the status of the individual who is beaten up affects the probability of retaliation. If he is influential, then there is a greater chance for retaliation than if he is a member of low status.

The second problem dealt with concerned the kind of group that is mobilized for purposes of retaliation. We found that the status of the Vice Lord jumped on is crucial in determining the kind of subgroup that will function as a raiding party. If the person is an important member of a section or has influence with an important section leader, then the section will function for retaliation; if the person has high prestige in the branch or influence with a member of high prestige, then the branch will be the retaliatory force; and finally, if the individual is one of the top Lords in the Nation, then the Nation will be mobilized for retaliation.

Other Contexts

We have identified "hustling," "wolf packing," "pulling jive," "meetings," and "shooting craps" as social contexts that form an important part of Vice Lord street life. While Vice Lords do not feel these contexts are as important as gangbangs, they are far more frequent in occurrence. Most of Vice Lord street life is comprised of such happenings.

Clique membership is the only affiliation that is actualized in the context of "hustling" and "wolf packing." "Hustling" is any activity other than legitimate employment that is aimed at making money. Begging in the streets, gambling, and stealing are common kinds of hustling activities. Although begging in the streets and gambling are usually individual activities, stealing often involves groups. Strong armed robbery, a form of theft, is often used in the ghetto to make money. While individuals do strong-arm alone, it is more usual for this to be done in groups since it increases the chances for success. Too large a group, however, would attract attention, and also cut down on individual profits. Thus a group between two to four is felt to be best suited for hustling purposes. Successful group strong-arming is also dependent upon teamwork. There is a division of labor—each person is allocated a specific task: for example, stopping the intended victim (usually by asking him for a cigarette, or for the time); grabbing hold of the victim; keeping the victim from struggling by threatening him with a weapon or striking him; and taking the victim's money and other valuables. Since teamwork is so important, individuals most often hustle with their closest friends—people whose abilities and limitations they know well. Therefore, it is clique affiliation that becomes actualized in hustling contexts.

"Wolf packing" is somewhat similar in form to strong-armed hustling. However, the aim is different. Strong-armed hustling is concerned with making money, while wolf packing is primarily for enhancing a rep. Wolf packing was explained to me in the following way: "Wolf packing—like for instance me and some other fellows go out and knock you down 'cause we feel like it. That's what it is. I might take your money, but I really want to kick some ass anyway, so I decide to knock the first thing in my way down." Vice Lords feel that for wolf packing, as for hustling, one must be able to trust the actions of others in the group. For this reason close friends usually wolf pack together. As one Vice Lord put it, "You pick peoples you know you can depend on—your close partners. See, if you pick someone you don't know, he liable to trick on you [tell the police], or run on you." Thus clique affiliation becomes actualized in wolf packing contexts, as it does in hustling contexts.

In the context of "pulling jive" (drinking an alcoholic beverage—usually wine) Nation affiliation is actualized. "Pulling jive" is one of the most frequently occurring social contexts in Vice Lord street life. Vice Lords pull jive before and after gang fights, following successful hustling, and while they are hanging on the corner. There is a certain pattern to the way Vice Lords drink wine. We shall look at this more closely in a later chapter. What is important here is that in the form of pulling jive which is the same for all Vice Lords, the unity of the Vice Lord Nation is symbolically stated. Before any wine is drunk, a portion is poured on the ground in the letters CVL. Vice Lords say that this is for all the Lords who have been killed or who are in jail. Further, a study of incidences of pulling jive shows that

Shooting crap in an alley off 15th Street; three of the boys belong to the 15th Street Lords and two are Ridgeway Lords.

any Vice Lord who happens to be present, regardless of clique, section, age group, or branch affiliation is offered some wine to drink, and, therefore, takes an active part in the drinking activity. Thus it is apparent that Nation membership is the crucial group affiliation in the context of pulling jive.

"Meetings" are a social context in which Nation, branch, section, and age group affiliation may be significant. Clique membership is never actualized in this context. There are regular periodic meetings of the entire Vice Lord Nation that are presided over by the most important leaders of the club. Any Lord in the Nation can come to these meetings. At meetings of the Nation that I attended there were between a hundred, and a hundred and twenty-five Vice Lords present. Branches, sections, and age groups also hold meetings at various times. However, there is no regularity to these meetings. Usually, they are held only during times of crisis—for example, following some kind of incident that could lead to a gang fight.

Although "shooting craps" is a frequent Vice Lord social activity, it forms a social context in which Vice Lord street life cuts across the more inclusive street life of the Lawndale community. While Vice Lords most often shoot craps with other Vice Lords, membership in the club is not significant in this particular context. Anyone with money, regardless of clique, section, age group, branch, and even club membership is welcome to take part in the game. In crap games I observed there were middle-aged men, as well as Vice Lords, actively participating. A Vice Lord explained this to me in the following way:

> Whenever everybody get some money, we get together and shoot some dice. I mean the whole hood. This don't mean just the Vice Lords, it means anybody in the neighborhood—anybody got some money, women, babies, kids. If you got some money, we'll know you.
> So we get a crap game on 15th Street, and somebody else got one on 16th. You, me, him, we all over on 15th Street. We going to shoot dice among each other. And if one man bust all of us, he know there's a game on 16th, and he going down there and try and bust them. See, you go anywhere the money is.

In this chapter our interest was focused on one aspect in the pattern of Vice Lord social interaction—the relationship between social contexts and groups. We had previously noted that Vice Lords belong to a series of groups. We then asked when is membership in one, rather than another, of these groups activated? We found that the activation of group membership is systematically related to particular social contexts. This systematic relationship forms part of the pattern of the Vice Lord social system. In the following chapter we shall look at another part of this pattern.

4

The Social System—Roles

AN IMPORTANT PART OF THE PATTERN in Vice Lord social life is comprised of what can be called social roles. In our study of Vice Lord roles we shall use a theoretical framework to help organize and bring sense to the data. Dr. Allen Hoben has written a concise explanation of the role concept in a community study guide for Peace Corps volunteers. Part of this will form a section of our framework, and that portion of his work is included here.

Hoben identifies three general aspects of social roles:

First, there are in any society a number of well-defined and publicly recognized social personalities or identities. Father, son, teacher, pupil, employer, and employee are examples of social identities in our own society. It should be stressed that these are not different kinds of people, but different social identities. The same individual is called upon to assume different identities in different situations.

Second, in any society only in certain social identities can people interact with one another. There are very definite rules of combination—a sort of grammar of possible social interaction. For example, father-son, father-daughter, husband-wife, teacher-pupil, and employer-employee are grammatical combinations of social identities in our own society. Father-pupil, employer-son, daughter-teacher, and son-wife are not. A single social identity (father or professor) may have a grammatical relationship with several other identities (father-son, father-daughter, or professor-student, professor-professor, professor-chairman of department).

Third, there are in any society, for each grammatically possible combination of social identities, agreed-upon rules concerning appropriate modes of interaction. This means, for example, that father and son, teacher and pupil, employer and employee are aware of the behavior they expect from one another [Hoben 5–6: n.d.].

If we focus on the third aspect—the "agreed-upon rules concerning appropriate modes of interaction"—differences in kinds of rules are found:

1. There are formal rights and duties limiting the behavior of individuals in identity relationships. A Vice Lord who assumes a particular identity expects certain

rights, and owes certain duties to the Vice Lord who assumes the alter identity in the relationship. If either party fails to fulfill his duties, sanctions are imposed.

2. There are modes of behavior that are considered proper between individuals in social relationships. These we can call social etiquette.

3. There are modes of behavior that signal which identities are being assumed.

The final point in our framework concerns role distribution. If the distribution of roles in relation to social contexts is studied, important differences in contextualization are found. While Vice Lords assume some identities in a few contexts, there are, in contrast, other identities that are assumed in a wide range of social contexts.

Vice Lord–Vice Lord

The role Vice Lord–Vice Lord is found in a wide range of social contexts. Whether hanging on the corner, drinking wine, or gang fighting, individuals in the club often assume the identity Vice Lord in relationships with each other. There are a certain set of rights and duties that regulate behavior between individuals assuming this identity. When my informants discussed the way Vice Lords should behave toward one another, the idea of mutual help was a constantly recurring theme. As one person put it, "We may get to arguing and then humbug [fight], but soon as it's over we buy a drink, and we back together. See, the way we see this thing, we all out to help each other . . . really."

Mutual help can be divided into two kinds—help with regard to material things, and aid in fighting and other dangerous activities such as strong-arming. Vice Lords state that members of the club should help each other in any kind of dangerous activity. If a Vice Lord is jumped on by members of another club, all other Vice Lords present should help, regardless of personal risk. Also, if a Vice Lord asks another to help in hustling, he should not turn down the request. When I asked if most Vice Lords actually do usually give physical help to each other, the answer was an emphatic "yes." For example, I asked one Vice Lord what one should do if he saw another Lord getting jumped on. The answer was, "Help him! You not supposed to do this, you going to do this! You a Lord . . . Lords don't fear nothing but God and death. I never seen a Lord cop out [chicken out]—not a true Lord." When pressed, however, some informants admitted that not all Vice Lords act in this manner. Those who don't, however, are strongly sanctioned. A person who does not fulfill the obligations of physical support is derisively referred to as a "punk," or a "chump." According to one informant, if one is judged a punk, other Vice Lords will refuse to have anything to do with him: "They say he's a punk—tell him to go on away from them; tell him to go home; tell him to stop hanging with them." Another Vice Lord stated that a person would actually be physically sanctioned if he "punked out": "Most of the time when a fellow punks out they wait until the person get out of the hospital, get his side of the story, see did the dude really punk out. If

A group of Vice Lords "hanging" on the northeast corner of 16th and Lawndale.

the guy say he punked out on him they usually jump on him . . . or take him in Cobra territory and put him out."

It should be pointed out, however, that the obligation of physical support is similar to the commandment "Thou shall not kill." Although this commandment is supported by sanctions, there are certain circumstances when it can be broken with impunity. Sanctions are not imposed for killing in self-defense, or during a war. Similarly, sanctions are not always imposed on Vice Lords who do not give physical aid to other Vice Lords. For example, if a small group of Vice Lords is attacked by a much larger enemy force, it is felt that one Vice Lord should run and get help rather than stay and help the others. Also if a Vice Lord sees another member being beaten up by an enemy group, he can try to get a weapon before helping in the fight. Even if he returns with his weapon after the fight is finished he will not normally be sanctioned for punking out. There are also situations where a Vice Lord's obligations to help other Vice Lords in hustling activities is put aside. For example, at 3:00 A.M. one morning two drunk Vice Lords came to the house of Doughbelly and yelled in his window asking him to help them hold up somebody. Because of the noise they created Doughbelly's mother told him he could no longer live in her house. He became enraged at the two drunk Lords for getting him "thrown out," and told them he would not help them, and further, if he saw them again he would kill them. It was never suggested publicly that Doughbelly had punked out for re-fusing to help in this situation, and no sanctions were imposed.

Since there are sanctions imposed for failing to fulfill the obligations of physical support, it seems clear that these are part of the rights and duties of the Vice Lord-Vice Lord role. A Vice Lord has the duty to give physical support to other Vice Lords and the right to physical support from other Vice Lords. This set of rights and duties, however, can be tempered by particular circumstances.

The rights and duties of mutual help regarding material things presents a more complicated picture. Although Vice Lords say they should lend money and clothes, share food, and should not try to "beat" (con) each other out of their possessions, many individuals admit that most do not usually act in this way. In fact when I asked if Vice Lords usually do give material help, the answer was often hoots of laughter. In my observations I found that Vice Lords frequently tried to beat each other out of things, and saw many cases where individuals refused to lend things to other Vice Lords. There were no group sanctions imposed for failing to live up to this ideal, and when questioned, my informants stated that it was the responsibility of the individual who felt he was wronged to take what action he felt necessary. Can it be said that mutual help with regard to material things is not important in the Vice Lord-Vice Lord role? I don't think so. It is generally felt that individuals who refuse to live up to the ideal of mutual help should not deny the validity of the ideal. Further, there are situations when most Vice Lords usually will extend material help to other members of the club. If they are convinced that a member is really in need, then he usually will be helped. An individual may have been thrown out of his home by angry parents and have to fend for himself on the streets, or he may have recently returned from jail with no money and nowhere to live. In such cases other Vice Lords usually give whatever help they can. I observed an instance where material help was given to a Vice Lord in need. A set had been planned by the 15th Street Lords. Throughout the prior week, the set was a constant topic of conversation. The clothes that were going to be worn and the girls that were going to be present were repeatedly discussed. The evening of the set I met a group of 15th Street Lords at the house of Tex, the 15th Street's president. Everyone was dressed and ready for the set except Old Dude. Old Dude was one of the least important members of the 15th Street Lords. He was thought by everyone to be "light upstairs" (not too intelligent), and he did not have a rep for gang fighting. His family was extremely poor, even by ghetto standards, and his mother gave all her attention to another brother. One of the fellows asked Old Dude, "Say man, why you ain't dressed for the set?"

"I ain't got no pants. It's my own fault. I knew about the set all week, but I just ain't got no pants."

Tex said, "Damn Jack! You should've asked us. You a Lord—we take care of you." Tex then asked his mother to press one of his extra pairs of pants, and another of the fellows went home to get a clean shirt for Old Dude to wear.

It is interesting that in this context Vice Lord sanction individuals who will not help a club member in need. Such a person is referred to as "stingy" and becomes the topic of derogatory conversation. Certainly anyone with leadership aspirations could not afford to be classified as stingy. From this we can conclude that material help is a binding obligation when it is thought an individual is in real need.

Looking now at the rights and duties regarding mutual help, a clearer picture emerges. Mutual help, both material and physical, is a binding obligation when
Vice Lords feel real need is involved. If a Vice Lord is jumped on by members of
an enemy club, he is in danger of serious physical injury. When a Vice Lord has
nowhere to live and nothing to eat, he is also in need. The obligations of mutual
help become binding in such situations. We can now better understand why Vice
Lords feel that even when an individual is not in real need, it is still necessary to
uphold the value of mutual help. Life in the ghetto poses many risks; the rights and
obligations of the Vice Lord-Vice Lord role provide a kind of social insurance. No
one knows when he may find it necessary to bring into play the obligations of mutual help. Thus the ultimate legitimacy of such obligations must be jealously
guarded. Publicly denying that these obligations are legitimate would threaten the
well-being of all Vice Lords. Therefore, it is felt that individuals should not deny
the legitimacy of a request for help, although the request does not always have to be
granted.

There are certain forms in the interactive behavior of individuals who assume the Vice Lord identity that can be called social etiquette. Standardized greetings are one example. When individuals pass one another on the street there are
two greetings that are used. In some cases the right hand is raised to the side, the
hand balled into a fist, and the arm raised and lowered two or three times. In other
instances the club name is yelled out as a greeting.

Upholding the legitimacy of the obligations of mutual help is also a part of
Vice Lord social etiquette. For example, if a Vice Lord were asked to loan money to
another member and answered, "No man! I ain't your daddy. I ain't going to give
you nothing!" this would be a breach of good manners, that is, it would go against
social etiquette. It would also be interpreted as a hostile act—a signal not only that
he was refusing to assume the identity Vice Lord vis-à-vis the asker but also that he
was assuming an identity as a protagonist. The individual who asked for the money
would then have the legitimate right to retaliate by starting a fight, that is, public
opinion would support his starting a fight. In contrast, if the person asked for the
loan couched his refusal in the form of an excuse, and in a friendly tone, this would
constitute proper social etiquette. It would not be interpreted as a hostile act, and
public opinion would not support the asker if he started a fight. I observed an instance that provides a good example.

A meeting of the Nation had just occurred, and groups of Vice Lords were
standing around talking. I was with Goliath, my major informant, and a few other
Vice Lords. While we were talking, Tico walked up and said to Goliath, "Hey man,
give me a quarter. I get paid Tuesday, and I'll take care of you then, but I got to
get me some jive [wine] tonight." Goliath answered, "Yeah man, I'll take care of
you," and turned around and started talking to another Vice Lord who was standing
with us. After a few minutes Tico again asked Goliath for the money. "Damn Jack,
what about the quarter?" Goliath answered, "Yeah, I'll turn you on." This continued for a short time—Goliath kept assuring Tico he was going to give him a quarter, but made no move to actually do so. Finally he reached into his pocket, pulled
out some change, and began counting it intently: "Let's see, I need forty cents for a
Polish [sausage], twenty-five for a . . . "

"Shit man, we Vice Lords. We supposed to be brothers. Come on, Jack, I gotta get me a taste."

"I'll take care of you. You know that. Now I need forty for a Polish, twenty-five for carfare, fifty to get my baby some milk . . . shit! I'm fifteen cents short. Say man, can you loan me fifteen cents?" Tico shook his head, and walked away in disgust.

I should note that Goliath did not need 15¢—he had $10 in his wallet—but this was used as an excuse rather than denying that he should loan the quarter. Goliath was, therefore, observing the proper social forms of the Vice Lord-Vice Lord role. (Incidentally, Tico did not need the quarter. I saw him later that evening with $2.

Street Man–Street Man

Another role that is found in a wide range of contexts is what I call the Street Man-Street Man role. The social identity Street Man is one that all male Blacks living in the ghetto assume at various times. Vice Lords often assume this identity in their relationship both with other members and those who do not belong to the club. The essential element in the Street Man-Street Man role is manipulation. It is expected that persons who assume the Street Man identity will try to manipulate (or, as Vice Lords say, "beat") each other out of as much as possible. This manipulation, however, has certain bounds set to it. An example will illustrate.

While driving down 16th Street, Cochise was hit by a woman who had gone through a red light. She did not have insurance, but agreed to pay $40 for damages. After two weeks she still had not paid Cochise, and he decided to get the money himself. He asked Jesse, another Vice Lord, to accompany him and help out in case of any trouble. Jesse was to get a share of whatever was collected in return for his help. Jesse and Cochise broke into the woman's house and took a television set, radio, and toaster. Cochise kept the toaster and radio. Jesse got the television set, but gave Cochise $20 so that each would have a fair share. Later Cochise and Jesse were on the corner of 16th and Lawndale discussing what had happened. Cochise mentioned that he was going to take the radio home and then try to sell it the next day. Jesse said, "No man, don't do that. The Man liable to come in your house, and if he find the radio he'll bust [arrest] you. Now I know an old building, ain't nobody in there. You can leave it there." Later, when I mentioned this incident to Goliath he laughed and said, "You know why Jesse said that?" I said, "No."

"Well, if Cochise took that radio home, Jesse couldn't go in his house and get it, but if he put it in that old building then Jesse'd sneak back at night and get the radio hisself."

In this instance Jesse was attempting to manipulate Cochise in order to beat him out of the radio. According to the expectations of the Street Man-Street Man role it was acceptable for Jesse to attempt this. However, there are limits to the ways it could be done. If Cochise had taken the radio home, it would not have been acceptable for Jesse to have taken it from there. Stealing from the home of a close acquaintance is considered wrong behavior by Vice Lords, and few individuals would have much to do with a person known to act in this way. On the other hand, if Jesse could have talked Cochise into leaving the radio in an abandoned building, he would have been free to go back and get it for himself. Successfully manipulating others is called "whupping the game." If Jesse had been successful in whupping the game on Cochise, his prestige with other Vice Lords would have increased. It is now possible to isolate at least one of the rights and duties of the Street Man-Street Man role. Individuals who assume the identity Street Man have the right to expect others in the alter identity will follow the rules which set limits to manipulation, and have the duty to follow these rules themselves. The sanction of public opinion supports this right and duty.

The social etiquette of the Street Man-Street Man role consists of greetings, farewells, and forms of ongoing social interaction. There are two greetings that are generally used. An individual may say either "How you doing?" or "What's happening?" Sometimes "man" or "Jack" is placed at the end of the greeting—for example, "What's happening, Jack?" The person who begins the exchange has the option to choose the greeting he wishes. When one of these greetings is used to initiate a social exchange, the other is usually the response. To terminate a social episode most individuals say simply, "Later."

A form of behavior that is a part of ongoing social interaction is hand slapping. In hand slapping a person puts his hand out with the palm up, and another person touches the open palm with his own hand or arm. Although this might seem somewhat similar in outward form to shaking hands, as we shall see, it has radically different social significance. (Vice Lords do not usually shake hands like most middle-class Americans.)

A hand-slapping exchange can begin in two ways. In some cases during the course of a social episode an individual puts his hand out with the palm raised. The proper response is to touch the raised palm with a hand or arm. Other times a hand-slapping exchange is initiated by a person raising his hand with the palm down. The proper response is to put out the hand with the palm raised. The first individual then slaps the outraised palm. In the first kind of hand-slapping exchange there are several kinds of responses to an outraised palm that are considered proper. Some, but not all, of these have different social significance. A person can respond to an outraised palm by slapping it with his own palm either up or down. This has no particular social significance. Touching the outraised palm with the arm or elbow is also a possible response. Further, an individual can vary the intensity of his slap. These last two differences—touching the palm with an arm or elbow rather than the hand and varying the intensity of the slap—do have significance.

In general, when a hand-slapping episode occurs during social interaction it emphasizes agreement between the two parties. If an individual has said something, or done something he thinks particularly noteworthy, he will put out his hand to be slapped. By slapping it, the alter in the relationship signals agreement. Varying the intensity of the slap response indicates varying degrees of agreement. A Vice Lord may say, "Five Lords can whup fifty Cobras!" and then put out his hand, palm up. Another club member responds by slapping the palm hard, thus indicating strong agreement. The first Vice Lord might then say, "I can whup ten Cobras myself!" and again put out his hand. This time, however, the second individual may respond with a much lighter slap. This indicates that he does not emphatically agree with the statement. If he barely touches the outraised palm with a flick motion of the wrist he indicates disparagement. However, if he touches the outraised palm with his arm or elbow this shows that he respects the person, but does not feel his statement is either particularly true, or else particularly important. If the second individual raises his hand before the first puts out his hand, this not only emphasizes agreement, but also expresses esteem.

It is considered a serious breach of social etiquette to purposely ignore the initial moves of a hand-slapping episode. I was told that to do so is a serious insult. While I observed several instances in which Vice Lords indicated disparagement by lightly touching an outraised hand with a flick of the wrist, I never saw anyone refuse to respond at all in some appropriate way.

Vice Lord–Enemy

The social identity, Vice Lord, has a grammatical relationship with the identity I call Enemy. An individual who is a member of the Vice Lords can assume either the identity Street Man or Vice Lord in social interaction with males who are not members of the club. If he assumes the Street Man identity, the grammatically proper identity for the alter to assume is also Street Man. However, if he assumes the Vice Lord identity, then the alter is automatically defined as an Enemy. Both parties in such a relationship have an initial option as to which identity they will choose, but if either chooses the identity which defines the situation as one of enmity, then the other must choose the grammatically matching one. In other words, if the individual who is not a member of the Vice Lords assumes the identity Street Man, then the person who is a Vice Lord has an option. He can assume either the identity Street Man, or that of Vice Lord. If he assumes the latter, then the first individual must act as Enemy. In contrast, if the first individual assumes the Enemy identity rather than that of Street Man, then the second person must assume the identity Vice Lord.

Although there is insufficient information to discuss the Vice Lord-Enemy role in terms of rights and duties and social etiquette, I did find both behavioral expectations between individuals interacting in this role and regularized forms of behavior that signal the assumption of the identities in question. There are two kinds of behavior that are expected in situations of enmity. Vice Lords call these "whuffing," and humbugging. Whuffing is the exchanging of insults and challenges to fight, while humbugging is actual fighting. Not all situations of enmity end in humbugging. Individuals who assume the identities Vice Lord and Enemy, respectively, can play out their social interaction solely in terms of whuffing.

People who intend to assume the identities which define a social situation as one of enmity do not signal this simply by initiating physical violence. There are certain verbal formulas which indicate a person is assuming the enmity identities. One of the most common is to demand a sum of money—for example, "Hey man, gimme a dime!" When put like this, it is not an actual request for money. If a dime were given, then a demand for more money would be made until finally the individual would have to refuse. Refusing the demand is the cue that the alter is assuming the grammatically matching identity of enmity, and from there the relationship can be played out in terms of whuffing or humbugging.

Another formula for signaling the assumption of an enmity identity is to start an argument. Individuals often argue in the course of social interaction, and these arguments do not always signal enmity. However, when an individual starts a violent argument over something that is considered extremely inconsequential, it does function as such a signal. For example, an individual may be talking about the kind of clothes he likes the best. If another person begins to vehemently argue with him, it is a sign that he is assuming an enmity identity. Of course it is not always clear whether an argument is "consequential" or not, and there are other subtle cues which also indicate if an identity of enmity is being assumed. My informants, however, could not verbalize about these. They said, "Man, you just *know* . . . that's all." Unfortunately, during the time of my field work I was not able to make a systematic study of these subtle cues. Possibly, they consist of such things as facial expressions and certain qualities and tones in the voice. Not all people are as adept at appropriately responding to such cues as others. Being adept at responding properly is one of the things that constitutes "knowing what's happening," or, as Cupid puts it in Chapter 6, "knowing how to live on the streets."

Leader–Follower

There are several named leadership identities that are assumed in a few social contexts. We have already discussed these in Chapter 2, and it is not necessary to deal with them in detail here. However, in order to be eligible for these identities—for example, President, War Counselor—one must be what Vice Lords call a "Leader." We can, therefore, discuss a Leader identity without necessarily specifying a formal political position. Vice Lords define a Leader as a person who has followers. To a person outside the world of the fighting clubs this may seem overly simplistic, but what defines one as a Leader or Follower is self-evident only to Vice Lords. There are several reasons for this. Leadership is highly contextualized—that is, there are few contexts when an individual's identity as Leader emerges. Further, the same person may assume identities of both Leader and Follower at different times.

A few definitions would help clarify the discussion. A Leader is one who exercises power. Power is the ability to get others to do one's will. The exercise of leadership is thus the exercise of power. Among Vice Lords a person is recognized as a Leader when he has the ability to get others to do his will. In some societies power is often a function of force. Individuals exercise leadership through the use, or threat of use, of physical or mystical force. This fits the popular conception of the gang leader. Among Vice Lords, however, power is not based on force. A Leader exercises power through what we can call influence. Vice Lords follow others because they like them, or respect them, or because they think they will gain something by doing so, but not because they fear them.

What are the contexts in which the Leader and Follower identities are relevant? There are two kinds of contexts when people assume Leader and Follower identities—that is, there are two kinds of contexts in which power is exerted. The first kind includes situations that demand physical action. Some obvious examples are: gangbanging, wolf packing, and hustling. An example from the 15th Street Lords provides a good illustration. I had met Tex, the President of the 15th Street Lords, several times before I found out how important a person he was. Observing Tex riding in a car, hanging on the corner, or drinking wine, there was no clue that he was a person with power. He was not particularly assertive, and when demands were made of him, he usually complied. If there was an argument over who was going to sit by the window while we were riding, Tex usually lost. If there was an argument over who was going to buy cigarettes, Tex usually lost. At a party one evening a group of 15th Street Lords stole a large sum of money from an individual who was not a member of the club. When Tex tried to get them to return the money, he was completely ignored. Then one evening there was a fight between a 15th Street Lord and a member of the Cobras. Everyone expected the Cobras would attack 15th Street territory. In this situation Tex's identity as a Leader became relevant. He immediately took charge of planning for the defense of the territory. Not only were his orders obeyed without question but individuals sought him out to ask what they should do.

I observed other instances which also demonstrated the pattern. Crow was one of the top Leaders in the Nation. Next to Cave Man, he was considered to be the most influential Vice Lord. I was on the corner of 16th and Lawndale one night with Pico talking to Crow. There had been an outbreak of fighting between the Lords and the Roman Saints that evening, and it was expected that the Roman Saints would attack 16th and Lawndale. Pico suggested that he lead a group of Lords into Roman Saint territory, but Crow felt he should stay and help protect the corner. Pico did not even put up an argument, but simply said, "Yeah man, I guess you're right." Another time I was riding with Pico down Lawndale. We pulled up to a corner where there was a group of Lords. Crow was standing in the group, and Pico wanted to talk to him. Pico yelled out the window, "Hey Crow, you skinny mother fucker, get your ass over here!" Crow smiled and said, "What's happening man?" and walked over to the car.

These two examples help us better understand how Vice Lord leadership works. Both Tex and Crow assumed the identity Leader in the gang-fight context, but at other times assumed different identities. The casual onlooker observing their behavior at these other times might think they were not Leaders. He would be wrong. Both Tex's and Crow's failure to exert power in these situations was unrelated to their identities as Leaders since these were social contexts where the Leader-Follower role was irrelevant.

The second kind of context in which leadership identities are relevant are those defined by public decision making. Some decisions which affect the club are made during discussions between Vice Lords while hanging on a corner or in an alley. Usually, however, public decision-making takes place during club meetings. These meetings form an arena for leadership competition and demonstrations of power. A major objective of individuals who either are recognized Leaders or have leadership aspirations is to prove they have power—that is, to demonstrate that others will follow them. Many times the particular decision under discussion is secondary to this objective. For example, Cave Man had long been president of the Nation. During the summer of 1966, however, a group of the Senior Lords met and decided it would be best for the club if someone else took over. Cave Man agreed to step down and let Lonzo be the new president. At this time the executive board was instituted. Cave Man was not even given a place on the board, but was relegated to the formal position of a regular member. However, Cave still had considerable power, and lost little time in demonstrating it to the new officers. A group of social workers and clergymen from the West Side contacted Lonzo, the new president, to request permission to attend a meeting. They desired to get Vice Lord participation in a project. Several board members told them their request would be submitted to the club, but that the board would support it. When the meeting began, it was evident there was considerable opposition to this group. Cave Man had been hired by the YMCA to help control gang fighting, and had worked in close cooperation with a social worker who was part of this group. At the meeting, however, he was the loudest voice in the opposition. He said, "What have them social workers ever done for us? Shit man, we don't want them in here!" Cave Man became the rallying point for the opposition, and was able to marshall enough support so that the group was not allowed in the meeting.

After the formal part of a meeting it is customary for Vice Lords to congregate on 16th and Lawndale to drink, sing, and recount past exploits. After this particular meeting, Cave Man called out to Vice Lords who were standing around in small groups:

> Come on! We're going to tear up this West Side! We're going to tear down all these signs! [Someone had painted "Black Power" on several buildings.] We're going back to the old days! We're going to gangbang! Those Cobras and Roman Saints, They ain't shit! We're going to run 'em out of the West Side! Vice Lord! Vice Lord! Terrifying, terrific Vice Lords! This whole West Side belongs to the Vice Lords! Come on, let's go!

With that, Cave started out for 16th and Lawndale, and about 25 other Vice Lords fell in behind echoing his yells and shouts.

Cave Man's actions, both during the formal meeting and immediately after, can be understood in terms of the way Vice Lord leadership operates. He opposed allowing the YMCA worker to attend the meeting even though he was getting money from the YMCA and had in the past closely cooperated with this same person. He stated that social workers had never done anything for the club, but he had been instrumental in getting Vice Lords to cooperate with YMCA programs. For some time he had been working to limit gang fighting, but after the meeting called for a resumption of gang wars. All this makes sense if we look at Cave Man's position at this time. He needed to demonstrate that while he was no longer a formal officer, he was still a Leader—that it, a person with power. He needed to show that others would still follow him. An important segment of the new officers had tacitly agreed to letting the outsiders attend the meeting, but many members were against it. This gave Cave Man his opportunity. By mobilizing the resistance and successfully opposing the new officers he convincingly demonstrated his power to everyone. His later behavior is also understandable in these terms. Arriving at 16th and Lawndale in full view, at the head of a large group, further emphasized Cave Man's ability to gather a following. I do not believe he seriously intended to lead Vice Lords in a new gang war. He simply used an appeal to gang fighting values that are seldom, if ever, publicly questioned to gather a following and validate his identity as a Leader. After Cave Man reached 16th and Lawndale at the head of this group, he made no further move toward initiating gang fighting.

Some Vice Lords who are considered Leaders sometimes assume Follower identities in certain situations. There is a formal hierarchy of leadership positions that partially accounts for this. For example, the president of the Nation is thought to be a higher position than president of a branch. Therefore, the president of the Nation assumes the identity Leader in certain situations, while presidents of branches are Followers. The *de facto* distribution of power, however, fits only partially with the formal hierarchy of political positions. The incident just discussed involving Cave Man provides a good example. Bat Man was a Leader and vice-president of the 15th Street Lords. In the meeting of the Nation he opposed allowing the social workers to attend. Cave Man, even though he had no formal political position at this time, assumed the identity Leader in the meeting and Bat Man, who was a vice president, assumed that of his Follower. After the meeting, Bat Man joined the group that followed Cave Man to 16th and Lawndale.

The composition of a Leader's following changes in various situations. One time a Leader may join the following of another Leader (and bring his own following with him), but another time oppose that same Leader. Thus Vice Lords never know ahead of time exactly who will be allied and opposed in any particular instance. In other words, the strength of an individual's power is subject to constant fluctuation. We can now better understand why situations in which public decisions are made are contexts for the exercise of power. Power is based on the number of one's followers, but a Leader's following is constantly changing, and the exact extent of a person's power is not usually known. In situations where public decisions are made, however, lines of opposition are drawn, and power becomes crystallized. In the decision-making process individuals make the choice whether to assume a Leader or Follower identity. Those who choose the latter make the further choice as to whose following they will join. Through these choices power is actualized, and claims to the Leader identity are validated.

In this chapter we have concentrated on social roles—one aspect in the pattern of Vice Lord social behavior that comprises the social system. We have identified certain social roles and discussed these in relation to a particular theoretical framework. In the next chapter we shall switch our concern and look at Vice Lord behavior in terms of a cultural system.

5

The Cultural System

V ICE LORDS DEFINE THEIR WORLD and guide their actions in terms of a particular ideological framework. This constitutes Vice Lord culture. Our concern in this chapter is to describe some of the beliefs and values comprising
this framework, and to show how they relate to social behavior. I found four general
ideological sets which constitute Vice Lord culture. They can be designated: heart
ideology, soul ideology, brotherhood ideology, and game ideology. Each of these sets
functions to divide Vice Lord reality into a number of compartments we can call cultural scenes, and to guide and judge behavior within these scenes.

Heart Ideology

A Cobra swung on one of the fellows, and he come down with his knife out. That
means he's not scared to take that man's life if he wished to. That's what you
call a lot of heart—not scared to go to jail and pay whatever the consequences is.

If a group of boys say, going to break into a store or truck, and I tell this boy
to do it and he does it, the people say he got a whole lot of heart—he not afraid
of anything. He'll just go on and do everything the other person tell him to do.

A person who got heart, he not scared to do anything. Like we break in a liquor
lounge or something, he not worried about being busted. He's game for it. Or like
we in a fight, and we outnumbered say four to two. This man will stand up there
and fight with you no matter what. If you all go down, he there with you. You
all both go down together.

If you don't show heart people call you a punk, and they don't want to hang
with you. A punk is a person who like get into a fight with somebody and he don't
fight back. Or like if say me and you and somebody else, we going to rob somebody, and one of us be scared and won't do it. Then they say he punked out.

From these explanations we can understand what Vice Lords mean by
"heart." It is apparent that generally "heart" means bravery, but it means more
than just this. It also means bravery in terms of being "game," that is, being willing

to follow any suggestion regardless of personal risk. Having heart contrasts with punking out. A person who acts in a cowardly way—that is, who is not "game" for any suggestion—is a punk. Vice Lords believe that having heart is good, while being a punk, or punking out is bad. Heart, in other words, is one of the values of Vice Lord culture.

The heart-punk contrast defines a particular segment of Vice Lord reality. If we look at the explanations given by Vice Lords, it is apparent that the heart-punk contrast is relevant to situations where there is personal risk. Individuals are judged in terms of heart ideology only in situations which involve personal risk, and thus these situations are set off as distinct segments of Vice Lord life. A further look at our Vice Lords' explanations shows a division in risk situations—those involving fighting, and those involving robbing. Vice Lords call fighting humbugging, and robbing hustling. Humbugging is further subdivided: fighting between rival clubs is gangbanging, fighting between individuals is humbugging, and fighting which results when a group of club members goes out to jump on anyone they can find is wolf packing. We can show this more clearly by constructing a typology comprised of contrast sets.

Personal Risk Situations				*Other Situations*
*Humbugging*₁			Hustling	
Gangbanging	Humbugging₂	Wolf packing		

Personal risk situations contrast with other situations. Within the former, humbugging₁ contrasts with hustling. Within humbugging₁ situations, gangbanging, humbugging₂, and wolf packing all contrast. I should explain the difference between humbugging₁ and humbugging₂. Vice Lords refer to all kinds of fighting as humbugging. A fight between a boy and his father, a fight between males and females, a fight between rival clubs, or any other kind of fight can be referred to as a humbug. However, Vice Lords further distinguish between kinds of fighting. Gangbanging refers only to fights between enemy clubs. When individuals wish to distinguish between fights involving two individuals and fights involving rival clubs, they refer to the former as humbugs and the latter as gangbangs. Thus humbugging means any kind of fighting when contrasted with hustling, but means only fighting between individuals when contrasted with gangbanging. Therefore, I have used humbugging₁ to designate fighting in general and humbugging₂ to specify fighting between individuals.

Situations which involve humbugging₂, gangbanging, wolf packing, and hustling form distinct segments of Vice Lord reality that can be called cultural scenes. The use of scene is an analogy to the scenes of a play. As the action of a play is divided into scenes, so the action of Vice Lord behavior is structured into units we can call cultural scenes. My data on humbugging₂, wolf packing, and hustling is too limited to provide a detailed description of the pattern of action that takes place within these scenes. We can, however, study the cultural scene gangbang in greater detail. In Chapter 3 we made the distinction between gangbangs that resulted from accidental encounters between members of an enemy club and those that involved prior planning. Here, we are concerned with the latter.

There are four phases in a gangbang. The first we can call the prefight gathering. Before actual fighting begins, Vice Lords meet in their territory to plan strategy. During this phase there is drinking, singing, shouting, and bragging. Besides planning strategy Vice Lords are emotionally preparing to face the dangers of actual fighting. The second phase is the confrontation between enemy clubs. During the confrontation the groups stand facing each other, while the two rival war counselors are in between exchanging threats and insults. When the rival war counselors begin fighting, the third phase begins. This we can call the encounter. During the encounter the actual fighting takes place. The final phase is the postfight gathering. During this phase Vice Lords again gather in their territory to drink and brag of their exploits. The following account illustrates in greater detail what happens during the second and third phases.

> Now a fight like this really looks funny when it starts, but it turns out to be terrifying. When it's just coming night is when most of the fighting occurs so if the Man come, then everybody can get away.
>
> You get a stick, or maybe a knife, or a chain. And some fools got shotguns. What you really do, you stand there and the counselors are the first ones up. You stand back and you wait and see if they come to an agreement and talk. Now everybody standing there watching everybody else to see what's going to happen. And all of a sudden maybe a blow will be passed, and if it is, a fight start right there. Let's say this is what happened. Now nine out of ten you know everybody in your club, or everybody who came with you. You standing just like you'd met in a crowd and you were talking. It's really almost a semicircle. You just standing there and you're looking—you're watching the counselor. And if a blow pass, automatically the first thing you do is hit the man closest to you. After that if things get too tight for you then you get out of there. If it look like you getting whupped, you get out. It's all according to your nerve. The first who runs, that's it right there. Naturally if you're standing there and you're fighting, and you see half the club starting to run, you know the other half going to run soon. All it takes is one to run and the whole crowd breaks up. That's how a club gets its rep—by not running, by standing its ground.

The beliefs and values of heart ideology underlie the action of the gangbang scene. Esteem among Vice Lords corresponds to rep. Rep, in turn, depends on how others judge one's behavior in relation to heart ideology. These judgments are made on the behavior that takes place during the second and third phases of the gangbang scene. Heart ideology is also important in the first and third phases of a gangbang. Here, the beliefs and values of heart are reinforced through expression in ritualistic behavior. The basic tenets of heart ideology are contained in a poem composed by several of the original members of the club:

> From back out to south came the King of the Gestapoes, Lord of the Sabotage, Ruler of the Astronauts, knocking down fifty-sixty lanes.
>
> I say, for any man make attempt to take a Vice Lord down, he got to first find a rock to kill Goliath, overturn the pillars of Sampson, name the stone that David stood on, name the three little children that walked the burning fires of hell, stand in front of the Lord and say, "I have no fear."

> For the Vice Lords, I say for all Vice Lords, sixty-two across the chest, don't fear nothing, God and death, got a tombstone opportunity, a grave-yard mind, he must be a Vice Lord 'cause he don't mind dying.
> Vice Lord! Mighty Vice Lord!

During the first and third phases of a gangbang this poem is repeated by members of the club. The group divides intself into sections and each repeats alternating phrases. The final refrain—"Vice Lord! Mighty Vice Lord!"—is said by the entire group. In this manner the beliefs and values contained in the poem are given public expression, and heart ideology is reinforced.

Soul Ideology

There are several aspects to the Vice Lord concept of "soul." In one sense it refers to a general sort of Negritude. One who acts in a "hip" manner is said to have soul. However, it means more than this. Soul also refers to a way of doing something. When someone puts real effort into what he is doing, he is said to have soul. Stripping away superficiality and getting to the essence (or, in ghetto jargon, getting down to the real "nitty-gritty") is also involved in soul. Thus, for example, someone who sings with real effort and real feeling, and in so doing succeeds in capturing the essence of Black experience, has soul. His musical ability as such is irrelevant to the amount of his soul. Charles Keil has made an intensive study of the soul concept among Blacks in Chicago, and his research shows that the Vice Lord meaning of soul is the same as that found in ghetto culture as a whole. For a deeper analysis of the soul concept the reader is referred to Keil's monograph *The Urban Blues*. For our purposes, however, it is only necessary to note these three elements—Negritude, intense effort; and stripping away superficiality, or getting down to the real nitty-gritty—for Vice Lords base their judgments of soul on these elements.

Vice Lords value soul. To tell someone he has soul is a compliment, while to say he has "a hole in his soul" is a definite criticism. There are certain social situations in which judgments are made in terms of soul. These are contexts involving music. Music is an extremly important part of Vice Lord life. Vice Lords closely follow the music from Chicago's Black radio stations, and are constantly singing the songs that are broadcasted there. Many have formed their own singing groups which hold regular practices and perform at certain times. Dancing is even more important in Vice Lord life. Almost all Vice Lords take intense pride in their dancing ability, and lose few opportunities to demonstrate it.

Vice Lords judge one another's singing and dancing in terms of soul ideology, and thus that segment of Vice Lord life in which singing and dancing is found is set off from other social situations. Singing and dancing are important activities in two Vice Lord scenes. These are called by Vice Lords sets and hanging on the corner. A set can be translated as a party. Vice Lords usually display their dancing ability in this scene, and it is here that judgments are made in terms of soul. Singing takes place in many situations. Riding in a car, or meeting at a member's house, are a few examples of when singing occurs. However, judgments about singing are

"Pulling jive," the person in the striped shirt is about to pour out a portion of the wine in the Vice Lord letters.

usually made during performances that take place while hanging on the corner. When large groups of Vice Lords gather on the corner of 16th and Lawndale, for example, various groups demonstrate their singing abilities, and soul judgments are made on these performances.

Brotherhood Ideology

We noted in the last chapter that the idea of mutual help is an important value in the Vice Lord cultural framework. Vice Lords often express this in terms of brotherhood. "Man, we're just like brothers" is an often-heard phrase. One Vice Lord scene in which the values of brotherhood are especially relevant is drinking wine. There is a special ritual to wine drinking, and through this ritual the values of brotherhood are expressed and reinforced.

A wine drinking scene is initiated when a small group of Vice Lords gathers and someone suggests having a taste, or pulling some jive. The next phase is gathering the money. The individual who made the first suggestion usually acts as collector. Everyone in the group donates what he feels he can afford. Often it is necessary to go around the group several times before enough money is collected. Vice Lords passing by are also asked to contribute money and join in the wine drinking activities. After the money is collected and the wine is purchased, the next phase of the scene begins. This consists of "cracking the bottle." The bottle of wine is given to one of the group, who points it toward the ground and strikes the bottom of the bottle two times with the palm of his hand. This cracks the seal. Next, a small portion of the wine is poured out on the ground either in the letters CVL, or simply the letter V. This is interpreted as a symbolic gift to all the Vice Lords who have been killed or who are in jail. Finally, the bottle is passed around to everyone in the group, and each drinks the same amount regardless of how much money he contributed toward buying the wine.

There are two aspects of the wine drinking scene that give expression to brotherhood ideology. The first is the wine that is poured out in the Vice Lord letters. Vice Lords place a high value on wine, and pouring out even a little is a form of sacrifice. This sacrifice is interpreted as a symbolic giving to other Vice Lords in need. Vice Lords who are dead and in jail can't get wine for themselves, but this way there is symbolically something for them to drink too. The second aspect that reinforces brotherhood values is the way the wine is distributed and the way it is drunk. Every person in the group is entitled to an equal amount of wine regardless of the amount of money he contributed. Each gives whatever he has or whatever he can afford, but all, as Vice Lords put it, "share like brothers" in the consumption of the wine. Further, the wine is drunk from the same bottle. Each person does not take his portion in a separate glass, but everyone drinks from the same bottle. To Vice Lords this sharing further symbolizes the unity and brotherhood between members of the group. Thus the wine drinking ritual expresses and reinforces the values of mutual help—the values of brotherhood.

Game Ideology

In our previous study of the Street Man–Street Man role we noted that in certain situations the ability to successfully manipulate others, or, as Vice Lords say, "whupping the game," is an activity which sets off a particular part of Vice Lord life. We can call this segment a "game." The way individuals behave during a game scene is judged by other Vice Lords in terms of game ideology. Individuals who are thought to be good at whupping the game are said to have a "heavy game," while those who are judged to be poor at this activity are said to have a "lightweight game." The technique one uses in whupping the game is called a "front," and the quality of various individuals' fronts is often a topic of conversation.

Various Vice Lords often tried to whup the game on me with various degrees of success. A few examples will help illustrate the kinds of situations that constitute the game scene. Washington was known for having a lightweight game. He was seldom successful in beating anyone out of anything, but was often taken himself for various items of value. His attempt to whup the game on me consisted of simply requesting money: "Hey man, can you give me a quarter?" My answer was, "Sorry Washington, I don't have it today." This exchange constituted a game scene in Vice Lord life.

Blue Goose, in contrast to Washington, was known to have a heavy game.

Once he convinced me that a group of older men who were not members of the Vice Lords were planning to jump on me. He assured me, however, that I had nothing to fear because he would see to it that they did not bother me. He made a big show of chasing two old wineheads who he purported were plotting against me down the street. A little while later he asked me to loan him 50 cents and a shirt so he could make his "gig" (job) the next day. Of course, in gratitude, I was more than glad to help in any way possible. Later I learned I had taken part in a game scene and had been the victim of a successful front.

Our focus in this chapter has been on the ideological framework that constitutes Vice Lord culture. We have identified four ideological sets—heart ideology, soul ideology, brotherhood ideology, and game ideology—and have seen how these sets function both to define Vice Lord reality and to judge behavior. In the next chapter we shall look at Vice Lord life from a different perspective, and view the Vice Lord world through the eyes of an actual participant by means of an autobiographical life history.

6

Cupid's Story

MY LIFE. I really can't tell about it 'cause I lived it. I was born on 29th and Prairie. I guess I lived there for quite a long time. The first place I can actually remember I lived was on Frontier. We had a little small house over there, and we lived there for about three or four years. Over there there's nothing but killing. It was just a regular routine.

We got a big family. I got six brothers, and I think three sisters . . . I ain't counted lately. You know how it is. If somebody asks you how many, it's hard to say. I was nextest to the oldest. My sister, she older than me. And you know, we was up mellow. Then everything started going bad.

The way things ran down, me and my brother, we actually grew real fast because we had whole lots of family problems. We didn't have the proper clothes to wear, and people used to laugh . . . at the way we was dressed, and this and that. And even the teachers gave us a hard time—which they do to a lot of peoples. We actually had a difficult time going to school 'cause we didn't have the proper clothes. And people would talk about us. You know, it was hard. The teacher even failed me one semester. I was actually ashamed to go home and tell my mother that I had got failed. My problem was I didn't care. See, I never did think about nothing but the family, and because I don't want to fail, that don't mean that I should let myself go. Life still should be lived.

At the same time my father started acting funny too. It seemed like he was separating from the family. He wasn't coming home proper. He was coming home maybe . . . but not like he's supposed to. See, the old man, he didn't have no job, and he left us to ourselves. Many nights we went hungry, and if we didn't go out and get it ourselves, we wouldn't eat. You dig? He wouldn't provide the food. Like many days me and my brother went out and sold boxes and found pop bottles. We actually hustled pop bottles and boxes and stuff to get something to eat. If we didn't find different things to sell, we wouldn't eat. The old man, I guess he didn't believe in, you know, growing up. He just didn't want to see us grow up. Maybe he just couldn't realize it, but instead of us growing like normal kids, we had to provide for the family when he wasn't there. Then my mother, she was fixing to have a baby. It was my youngest brother, Jerry. And behind that she was sick. She was pretty sick for about five or six years. She was on the verge of a nervous breakdown, but she had to get up out of the bed and take care of the family. That's how it was for a long time. She was sick pretty close to ten years.

My uncle, he stayed in the penitentiary. Me and him was tight. See, we're the only two black sheep of the family. We didn't know it then, but as it came out we were. His daughter, she a prostitute now. She be out on 63rd. I don't know where he is now. I haven't seen him in maybe ten or twelve years, and I haven't seen my cousin in a long time, but I heard she's on the corner. Don't nobody trusting her in they house neither. She'll take anything from anybody.

You know how things go along. Time pass. I got older, so we moved on the West Side. We moved to out to West Jackson. Then we was going to Jefferson. I stayed there 'til I graduated. It was pretty nice over there. I was in a little club called the Vandykes. When we moved in I just saw them on the streets and they saw me. I was a new boy at school, so I just started hanging around with them. They turned out to be pretty mellow. I was in the Midgets. We was small. Still we wasn't as powerful as the Lords because they had the Braves in that hood too, and they were kicking strong. The Braves and the Jew Town Cobras, they had going east on Roosevelt, all that up tight. We just had about three or four blocks from Damen back to Ashland. We didn't have a whole big section like the Lords did. But what was ours was ours. We kept things up tight. Least *they* did. I was too young to do anything. Then came the King Pipers. That was Tiny Tim and them.

We all going to school together and we all lived on the same street. We'd get together and talk, and we got into a lot of little trouble together . . . steal milk and stuff like that. Mostly we used to play baseball or basketball at the playground, or something like that. Sometimes we might fight Tiny Tim and them, and the project boys, they'd come over and we'd run them back. Other than that we didn't have too much to worry about because where we was there wasn't too much over there people wanted anyway. That was around '58 or '59.

After we moved from there, we moved over to Paulina, and I got busted for burglary. I broke into this store next door—me and a cat named James Walker. We had broken into this place two or three times. The last time we broke in we stole a hundred and thirty dollars, and we got a .25 automatic. I cut my hand on that too. So this cat that was with me, he tricked.[1] He got busted or something and he tricked on me. They got me that night about ten o'clock. I was in the bed. My sister, she called and we went to the back door. My mother was in the bed too. My mother was sick. So they came and took me away, and I stayed for a day or two. Then I came home and when I went back to court they sent me to the Audy Home for two weeks. That mother fucking Audy Home is a bad place to be. I guess it's the worst place in the city of Chicago! It not nothing right!! They served us some chicken, it was so salty and so bloody that you couldn't even eat it. Only thing you could actually get full of—if you was lucky—was if you could catch some bread. You know, they used to throw bread and stuff around the room, and if you could catch it you could eat it, and if you didn't, you just didn't eat. I think the welfare had that place

---

[1] Tricked: informed.

then. That was when that big trouble at Sheridan[2] . . . they was talking about that incident at Sheridan. They was beating boys and half feeding them and starving them and carrying on about the same time.

I don't know how I got through it, but I got through it. After I got home, the Board of Education, they served me into court for not going to school. See, I never did go to school during that time. I ditched school. O.K., after I got out of the Audy Home I went back to school and they kicked me out. They supposed to let me back in, but they didn't want to. That's when the Board of Education sent me back to court. After that I went to Parental.

Parental was mellow. But it's not like home. You just don't have your freedom. It's pretty nice, though. You all live in little cottages and everything. You got to go to school like you regular do, and when you come back from school, come back to your cottage, you could look at television, dance. And on some nights they had different activities like bowling and shit like that. I didn't stay there no time really . . . about four months.

While I was in Parental my mother and them moved, but I didn't know it 'cause she hadn't wrote me no letter. So when I supposed to leave they got in touch with my father on the job, and he came and picked me up. That's when we had moved over on the West Side on Sawyer—13th and Sawyer.

By the time I got back, that's when things really got going. The Lords were getting strong then. That's when the Lords was kicking! Now I was still going back out where I used to live, but I had met some partners in The Place, and they was in the Lords. Lots of Lords was going to school with me too. I was going to Marshall, and lots of the Lords from Roosevelt were going there at the time. That's when I joined. Now I wasn't with them when they first started up. I must of come in maybe a year or two afterwards.

We used to hang around Sheppard School, and we used to be down at Sully's. It's a little restaurant like. On a Friday we used to go around there after school, and we'd be out there playing records or something like that. Pretty soon I just wanted to be mellow like everybody else. And 'cause they was my partners I just didn't cut them loose.[3] So that's how we got together. That was when they was first drinking that Thunderbird,[4] and that's when the Commanches first came out.

Now I'd go to club meetings or something like that, but I wasn't doing much fighting . . . at first. In a way I was scared. But after I got to know everybody, it was just like anything else. When they went humbugging I went. We used to be over at this boy's house all the time too, and at that time I used to sing a lot. I was in a different branch anyway. We called ourselves the Roosevelt Lords.

Then from Sawyer we moved down on Lawndale and 18th. That's when I really was deeply involved with the Lords. See, the 16th Street Lords, on Lawndale and out around there, that's where we was doing all our fighting. That's when I came in contact with everybody around there.

The night we moved out there, me and a stud named Horse—he got busted

---

[2] Sheridan: the name Vice Lords use for a reformatory for boys.
[3] To cut loose: to end the friendship.
[4] Thunderbird: a kind of wine.

for murder 'cause he killt this girl on Central Park—we went around and broke in somebody's house. I don't know how I got involved in it. We didn't get busted or nothing like that. So after he broke in and got the money we went around there and he got some wine. We came back and set on the porch and started drinking—all night and all day. I sat up on the porch and went to sleep, and when I woke back up, there were some more of the fellows. And pretty soon I got to know everybody, and everybody knew me. My partner from Parental, he cribbed out around there too, and me and him was pretty tight. He's called Count Dracula. He's dead now. Some broad shot him over fifty cents. So I started hanging around with them. Altogether there was twelve in our little group. There was Moon, Count Dracula, Pork Chop, Apache, Fool, Gowster Dan,[5] Duck, Chico, and some more fellows. When I first started they used to call me Little Fool . . . after this other stud Big Fool. He used to be a boss maniac, and I used to do what he did all the time. So they called me Little Fool. Then they used to call me Roughhead. I don't know why they called me that. Then from Roughhead they called me Cupid.

It's funny . . . the way I got my name. See, I was small. I was much smaller than I am now, but I was doing a lot. You know, not hand to hand, but I was a good man with a shotgun or a pistol. I was pretty good at hand to hand combat too because I know on occasions we didn't have no guns, and we still won. Anyway, we was coming down 16th street, and we was talking to some girls.

So this broad said, "Yeah, I know you. You sound like Cupid!"

And Gowster, you know how he is. Always likes to kid and carrying on. Gowster come around talking, "Yeah! Yeah! Look at this slick[6] Cupid!"

So that's my name. But I used to change my name myself 'cause the police used to be down my back a lot. Instead of running around dodging them I just changed my name. They didn't know no different. They don't know one person from another anyway. And somehow your name would get involved in a whole lot of shit, and that's when they'd get on to you. Just like that time they shot that man in the head. That night we had just got through fighting some Saints, and Fool, he was going to rob this man. The man said he don't believe they going to shoot him, so a stud name Charles, he shot him . . . shot him in the head. He got, I think twenty to sixty years. And my name come up in there.

I was in the St. Louis Lords when they started. You know, you didn't run around with a pack every day. Goliath and them, they had the Rat Pack, and you might see two of them today, and it would be different tomorrow. That's the way it is. You won't see no pack all the time. We called ourselves the St. Louis Lords. For officers we voted and everything. Dig? Moon was president. Now Moon and them was in jail at the time, and they wrote and told Apache to start our own group, The St. Louis Lords, so we started up. We was on 14th and St. Louis, down in the basement at Gowster Dan's. Apache was war counselor at first. Then they chose me. I don't know today really why they chose me to be war counselor.

O.K., if we going to fight we sit down, and we might discuss what's going

---

[5] Gowster: A style of dress—wide-bottomed pleated trousers, wide-lapeled coat, and so forth.
[6] Slick: good at conning people.

on. See, the way we had it, the office really didn't mean anything. Everybody need some kind of leadership, and everybody had just as much say as everybody else. It run something like Congress. That's the way we had it. We didn't have, like a certain officer to run the meeting. And when we were gangbanging, I couldn't say I really led them all because lots of them I missed out on. I wasn't there. You can't be with them all the time 'cause you never know who coming down there at you. The Lords didn't have to look for trouble. Trouble came to them . . . after they got their rep. See, a new club, they wouldn't go out looking for the Cobras. The first one they come looking for is the Lords. This is how the Lords got involved in lots of jive. People looked to them. Sometimes you don't have no reason why to go out and fight because when you get out there anybody might get killed. A small war just as big as a big war. It can become a big thing. Death is death you know. That's how it was.

Since we lived around there, we knew everybody. Everybody from that area know everybody. The majority of the Lords, we all know each other. Lots of them even know our families. So it was just like . . . brothership.

Now we created whole lots of stuff. We did whole lots, you know. We used to rob those peoples on the "L" all the time. We used to have a long sword, maybe three feet long, and we used to rob all those peoples and throw them off the "L." We usually started around Tuesday night. We used to do it from Tuesday to Saturday—go out on peoples and take they money and stuff. And any money we got we'd take and buy wine and get high, or else go down to the restaurant and buy some hamburgers and eat and fool around. Maybe we'd go out and bother somebody else, or go out to fight or something. We'd come back, get drinking, and get high again. That's all we did. It was a regular routine.

I guess the Lords had been going strong for about a year. But still I don't think they was as powerful then as they was in '61. After that things quieted down. That was the last year for humbugging and all that.

Now I was in the Midgets until I got out. What it was see, people draw this different thing, but we didn't go from Midgets to Juniors to Seniors. If they ask you what you was in, you always say Midgets. We Midgets, we always Midgets. Midgets was more . . . we had more respect. You would always have more respect for a Midget than you would a Senior . . . anytime. The Midgets always together. Now this was only for the St. Louis. I don't know how the other fellows did it.

The first club we were fighting was the Commanches. See, the Commanches were the Midgets for the Imperial Chaplains. They had changed their name to Commanches 'cause it had got too hot for them. And by then Cave and them had broke up most all the other clubs. Not Cave himself, but he was involved in breaking them up.

You know, nobody know for sure how a gang war starts. You never know if you even involved in a gang war at first. It could get started when you're not around, and you won't know nothing about it. One minute you may be down there, and the next minute you may be fighting. It could get started over a little simple thing. And what everybody really searching for is power. Like if I was to go out and start a fight with a club now. I wouldn't come back and tell my partners 'cause they may be mad at me, and when the humbugging starts they'd think it was this other club. So the Commanches could of started it and the Lords could have started it. Don't nobody know.

Now we was still fighting the Cobras at the same time. This one night we was just out having fun. We weren't out to shoot nobody in particular. I remember I had a .41 Magnum, one of my partners had a .38 special, and a stud had a .32 short. We went down Harding shooting up peoples. I don't know who we were shooting at, or what for, but we were fighting the Cobras, and I guess we were just shooting after everybody. We came back, and there weren't but two of us—me and Ringo.

So Ringo, he yells, "We're Vice Lords, mighty Vice Lords!" He yelling to this man coming up the street.

This stud said, "Well, you all Vice Lords, huh!?"

We said, "Yeah!"

And by the time he was reaching for his back pocket . . . I guess he didn't get out what he wanted to get out before I got what I got out. I shot him in the leg or foot or something, and he ran down the street . . . hollering like a dog! I don't even know if he a Cobra, but it was in the Cobra's hood. It was 13th and Avers, something like that.

But the Cobras came back on us. We was standing in front of the YMCA, and all of a sudden a car came around Polk street and started slowing down. Everybody turned around and looked.

I said to the man, "Go ahead, man! Go ahead!" But the stud wouldn't move his car. All of a sudden maybe about six studs popped out with shotguns, man, and Fool, he ran! He ran into somebody's crib, and he ain't knock on the door or anything! They chased us all the way down back to Independence!

One night we was coming from the Golden Dome. The papers said there were thirteen, but they only busted thirteen. They questioned everybody that was there, but they let me go. What happened, we asked this man for a nickel or a dime —something—and he got smart. This fool, Wine, asked the man for a nickel.

And he answered, "I ain't got no nickel."

Wine said, "You're going to have to give me a nickel!"

The stud said, "I'm not your daddy!"

The fool, Wine, said, "I know you're not my father!"

And Bull, he hit the man and knocked him down. The man tried to get back up. He was a judo expert. When he got back up again, I guess he was trying to get his position, and somebody hit him again. Boom! He went down. The poor soul, that's the last time he ever stood up . . . they stomped him to death. I forgot if he was dead on arrival or not. Anyway the people got forty years, fourteen, and twenty-five. Little Otis and them, they went to St. Charles. It was . . . you know, one of them things.

This is when we broke up the Commanches. After this one fight they broke up. It must of happened between nine-thirty and ten o'clock. I was sitting there on 16th and Lawndale, and some dude came down and said the Commanches jumped on Cave Man and some more of the fellows. I forgot who they was.

Somebody said, "Get everybody together!"

So somebody got on the telephone and called the fellows from Maypole—Tankson and them. We told the Vice Ladies to stay back, but they came down there anyway. I remember how this was—how we got down there. We all went on top of this big old truck. We was packed on it! So we came down there, and it seemed like it was really funny. We was down there . . . we was fighting, killing up each other, and all of a sudden we got hemmed up! And the Commanches, they had us! They had us up tight! We was boxed in. And so by some coincidence some of the fellows was coming behind them, but it just seemed like they wasn't getting there fast enough. And all of a sudden we looked up, and here come Tankson and them. So the Commanches, they seen them before we did, and they started running. I'll never forget this. It was King Solomon . . . crazy ass King Solomon. He had one of these little Hookvilles. It's a knife, a linoleum knife. Got a hook on the end. And a stud in the Commanches called Ghengis Khan, he went to run, and that's when Solomon got him . . . with the Hookville. Cut the stud's whole guts out! And two more of their fellows got shot—Big James, one of their top boys, and Big House Willy. We really fucked them up that night. This was the whole Imperial group, Commanches and everybody 'cause this was right on their corner, right where they grew up at, on 16th and Trumbull.

And Ghengis Khan was on the critical list. The paper made a big write-up on it. And they was talking about if Ghengis Khan would die, there was going to be a big war. But see, what they was trying to do was to turn up 16th and Lawndale and take over the corner. Naturally, we wouldn't go for that. And the police was after us that night too 'cause we was coming down the street—marching in the middle of the street with shotguns. It was a humbug.

I remember once we were in Washington Park, and lots of peoples was there. Count Dracula, he had . . . I think it was a .25 automatic. Peoples thought it was a German Luger—all them South Side clubs thought that. We almost had a little humbug, but nobody got hurt that day. It was just the respect we got. We got all of it. See, we went there for the Bud Billiken parade. Most all the City was there, most all of Vice Lord City went. But you know how it is, we just came out there with our partners. You see one of your partners so you go over there.

He going to say, "Well, couple more of the fellows over there."

So you go over there. Pretty soon you all together then. It never was a problem trying to find the fellows. It was easy. See, a Vice Lord had a certain kind of look. He looked like he was proud! He *was proud!* You could tell right now. If we walk out South or something, you know, they'd look at us and see a certain little something out of us that the Lords got. They was proud! They was proud of what they is.

So in Washington Park we were around some bushes, and some South Side boys, they got a urge . . . See they don't like for nobody to mess with their girls. We didn't know them. We was just out there messing with everybody. We was out there good-timing. And we all had our little jackets on. We had black jackets with white lettering across said St. Louis Lords. So we didn't have to say nothing 'cause our jackets was talking for us.

So they said, "You all Lords!"

We said, "Yeah! What about it?!"

They said, "Well a . . . we don't like Lords over here! Go back on the West Side!" or something like that.

So we said, "Well, we came for the parade, and we're going to stay 'til the parade's over with!"

Stud said, "Not if I can help it!" And he called his fellows—about three or four of them.

So they all started approaching us, and Count threw out that jive! They thought it was a Luger, and they ran. I don't think we shot nobody. I know we started shooting up the park, but the Man came around there so we went home. It had got too hot anyway.

I'd say Cave Man and them was kind of jealous of us, you know, 'cause at that time we was swinging pretty hard. We was younger than Cave and them. We was little bitty dudes, and they was big, but we used to keep pockets full of money. We used to keep gallons and stuff of wine. We always used to keep money and all stay clean while we had a suit or something on. And we used to have a house to go up all the time. We had got our own girls. We used to call them the Supreme Queens. They just did they part too. When we fought they was outside. They take our guns and hide them when the police bust us. They used to write to us in jail, and they was really something mellow. Lots of times if a certain fellow break in a store, some of the girls be with him. Just get different stuff. They was just like the boys. They used to drink just like we did . . . and maybe even more. They really came down to be pretty nice. And they used to give dances and stuff. We never did invite Cave and them because actually they was too old. They figured they was too old to be messing with us anyway. So we didn't never run up to them asking them for nothing. Everytime they came down they always wanted us to buy them something to drink, and they wanted our girls too. They were very jealous of our girls. And it all got messed up as soon as they found out about it. They wanted to come over and start tearing up things. They just couldn't let well enough be well enough. If the girls didn't want to go with them they wanted to start knocking them down, tearing up they houses. Pretty soon we didn't have anything anymore. We faced with the same problem, no place to go, and everything started all over again.

Another reason Cave and them was jealous of us was because we was independent, and them, they always wanted to run things. They wanted to be head of everything. Maybe they afraid they might get old. I don't know. But they wanted to run everything, and we didn't like it. So we changed our name to Mighty St. Louis Lords. And the YMCA was all over Cave because he supposed to be the leader and stuff. They gave Cave and them everything they wanted. They'd look to Cave before they'd look to us, and we was the ones out there creating everything. So we cut the YMCA and all them peoples loose, and we set up a kind of independent group. We had a sponsor of our own at the B.B.F.[7] But we was still Lords. Apparently they couldn't dig that. They wanted us to follow after them—you know, Conservative. Which we couldn't see why we should follow them, the Conservative

---

[7] B.B.F.: A social agency with social centers and street workers.

name, when we the only ones be out there doing anything. And we still didn't change our name. We stood up for ourselves, and now a lot more studs call theyselves Mighty Vice Lords too.

So then Cool Fool and King Solomon, they got into it with Cave and them. The same night Cave, Rifleman, and some more fellows, they came down, and they talking about how they going to fall on us 'cause we had got into it with Pole Cat, and we wasn't going by Conservatives. They got kind of hot, but we said we wasn't going to change our name regardless. We would fight anybody! And this was when the Roman Saints had just come out, and they had started coming across—moving north. The Saints had got heavy, and we was the only ones pushing them studs back. We had the Saints broke up. I ain't talking about these little studs around now calling theyselves Roman Saints. We went after their big boys. Their big boys was Kneecaps and them—all they presidents and stuff. They was scared to go to school. Really! If they did go the rest of them would have to come there and walk them home. We chased all of them home!

So Cave Man, he was out there talking about don't mess with them boys cause the boys weren't doing nothing. Now Count and me, we had built a rep then, so as soon as they seen we wasn't going to back down, they let us alone. See, the only thing they did, they all wanted the glory off other peoples. They wanted us to go out there and get beat up and shot all up, and they'd stand back and get the glory—talk about what they could do and never do it. That's the only thing they was good for then. Now maybe in their younger days they was swinging, but they weren't shit then—not anything, lots of wind. All they was doing, they come around and want us to buy them jugs and carrying on.

But when the shit come down and somebody doing the humbugging, only thing they going to do was say, "Well, you should go this way . . ."

Fuck going this way if you can't go with me! So that's the way it was. I guess we just weren't scared of them.

Hey! You know what? I used to hit some big fellows . . . bigger than me. I used to get a kick out of that. They thought they were stronger than me. I hated a big fat mouth more than anybody! Like Big James. I shot him with a pistol. Those gentlemen—lots of mouth! He'd go . . . I guess . . . if he was up tight.[8] And he was a boxer. He used to box in the Golden Gloves. Cherokee, he used to box too. He could have got someplace. Cherokee's a smart stud. He graduated from high school, and had a year of junior college. I don't know what wrong with the stud. He went completely down. I guess he just didn't have the bill to deliver. That's all. He had the ability, but he didn't want to. He wanted to stay young. Scared to get old. That stud about twenty-four now, and he still in the streets gangbanging. He a fool 'cause he'll go jump on somebody, and tell the people who he is, knowing he going to get busted.

Just like you go in somebody's pocket and take his shit and say, "I'm Cherokee! Remember that!"

And the police, that's just like him saying his right name. The police know exactly who it is, and where to go and get him. He got busted a lot of times like that. His folks are Muslims.

---

[8] Up tight: in this context "cornered."

I remember when we had that .22 rifle. The Saints hadn't been out too long. Like I said, the first time they came out we damn near broke them up 'cause they was scared to come to school. We had a big fight with them. There were three of us. And we whupped them in hand to hand combat. We had whupped them then, so they had broken down. Then the next thing, I heard the Roman Saints were carrying on.

We used to go down there and shoot up two or three of them all the time. They were scared. After meetings we used to go out and do things up in their hood. One night we had a meeting. It was Monday. We all was broke, and we couldn't buy no wine. So we went up there in the alley and started humbugging. I got shot in the leg that night. Yeah! We was coming down Albany, and they was shooting at us. We was running around, just having fun, though. We weren't running 'cause they was shooting. Well, there really wasn't anything else to do. We got in a gangway and hollered out, "Mighty Vice Lords!" and they started shooting at us again. I guess I didn't get out the way fast enough. I got shot in the leg. Matter of fact I didn't know nothing about it 'til the next day. My mother asked me how come I couldn't get out the bed. I thought I broke my leg or something. So I went to the doctor, and he took out a shell. He said I was pretty lucky.

We used to meet with the Roman Saints. The YMCA set the meetings up. But they didn't mean nothing. See, they never do sets it up for the peoples that're doing it. They always try to set them up with the people they think got the most influence. That's O.K., but the only thing wrong, they forget there's whole lots of jealous people. Everybody trying to be like that person up there. They figure if he goes to the meeting, why can't I go too when I'm out there standing by his side doing as much as he doing. That's what they thinking. But the Y, they just don't see it.

I went to lots of meetings myself. They cooked dinners and stuff. Had nice dinners. They'd dance and talk—talk about their difficulties . . . and that's it. They go back on the streets and go right on doing the old routine. Go back out there and start fighting again. It might last for a week. That's all. It don't last too long. Then they call another meeting. They talk about the same thing again. It's O.K. . . . I guess, but them peoples are not equipped like they should be. They don't have the right kind of anything. Maybe the money's out there, but the YMCA, they so strict. I don't see how you can be strict with a wolf pack. Really! You got to have a place of your own to really tear up something, like a gym or something.

And then lot's of peoples don't want to do one special thing. Like the YMCA, the only thing they want you to do is come up there and play some games or go in the gym and play basketball. Who wants to do that every two or three days? That's all it was. And not everybody can skate, so who wants to go there and skate? We better off everybody sticking together doing shit on the streets 'cause you was too limited to what you could do at the Y.

Then when they did have dances there'd be so many peoples there that you didn't know, trying to get something out of you, you better off not even going. Maybe they're trying to get some information for one of them pictures you see on television—like "Keep it Cool," and all them pictures. Anytime they going to have a dance at the YMCA you could bet after that that the Bell Telephone Company, or some movie outfit going to move in that next summer and try to make a picture of the group. They going to try to go around and meet everybody. Like last year them people come all the way from New York and all over just to meet us. And when we used to be fighting, they'd have peoples running up and down trying to get pictures out of it . . . to show how it was. It don't do no good! Peoples look at it and think you a fool! Those studs out there taking pictures, they don't even know what you doing it for. Actually they don't really care because they ain't going to give away nothing. You not going to get nothing out it! If they do give away something, its just to gain something themselves. To actually give something to somebody else you don't know is kind of foolish. I know I don't do it. I know the next man won't do it . . . especially if he think you not going to use it. Nine out of ten the money being donated, you don't get the proper use out of it anyway. Most of it go to waste.

But if they had just a little more than they have now, there probably wouldn't be many clubs out there. There going to be a club anyplace you go, and there always going to be a bad guy, or somebody that think they bad anyway. But when you got close to six hundred boys think they bad running down the streets carrying guns, that's pretty bad! And all these years they still haven't got no solution for this here problem. When you think of all the money the United States is spending out on other things, and they talking about this is not a major problem. I don't know what is! Something must be wrong. When you look at the future, the way everybody on the streets cutting up each other, there won't be no future! There won't be nobody left by the time they get through . . . to do anything. They killing off everybody! And the peoples, they don't care. Only thing they do is hire more policemen. What're the police doing? The police is killing more than we are! The police are living better than we are! They still driving five or six thousand dollar cars. I don't see how they can afford them. And most of us, we can't even afford a hamburger. They catch us with a quarter, they going to whup our asses up, take our quarter, and put it in they pocket. Yeah! And they say it's not a major problem! It is a major problem. But still when it comes up to the point, they always willing to draft you. You the first one they going to call for to fight. But they don't think they have to give you anything. Give you a decent place to go? Nope! You know, they might build a center or something, but they going to have so many rules there that you just can't enjoy youself. Like you're going to have only third nights to come. What good is coming on third nights, [when] you can't go every night? Not much good.

Then lots of places you got to pay to go. In some neighborhoods it's O.K. to pay, but in some neighborhoods everybody don't have that kind of money be paying. Around here if you haven't got that money to pay, you just don't go. All these centers just for the good guys anyway—good girls and boys. None of the clubs go in. Miss Love's center[9] is O.K., but she just don't have the money to run it, and the government hasn't given her any money. I guess it's too much like right. Yeah. Somebody might learn something! The more you stay down, the more they can rest.

---

[9] The Tennessee Memorial Community Center: Miss Love, a Black concert singer, donated her money and time to this center. There was no paid staff—only volunteers from the Black community. The center was one of the few places the Vice Lords were welcome. Miss Love was not able to get any funds from the War on Poverty, and the center closed for lack of financing.

The only thing they think is good for you is being busted. They treat you like animals! You're a savage . . . savage! As long as they can get you any time they want you, draft you and send you to fight something that they started, it's O.K. Huh! They start something they can't handle, they going to call you to go over and handle it. As far as them doing you justice, making sure that you got a decent place to go or a decent place to live, that's too much money they're got to be spending out. They can afford to give away millions of dollars a year to somebody else, but not to us. We got to be satisfied with what we got—making the best of it we can.

And around this Lawndale area there's more people starving than any China, I'll bet you—more people starving around here. Take this whole Lawndale area. I'd say ninety percent of them is on the Aid . . . some kind of welfare. In the morning you go out and there's somebody standing on their porch waiting on they check. That's why probably so many peoples on this ADC, carrying on. They look at everybody else. It's a common thing. Just like going to work now. You look like a fool not being on, and everbody else on, they're living better than you living and staying home. I don't know how they got it arranged, but its kind of foolish.

That summer of '61, that was the last summer of fighting. Then Cave and them faded out, and the 16th Lords was the Rat Pack . . . until we came and showed them who was boss. See, King Solomon and them broke up, and then we took over. We handled things. At that time I guess everybody else had kind of got away from the group. The old 16th Street, they didn't have no kind of influence. They didn't have nothing to say to us. We ran 16th Street! We *was* the 16th Street Lords, actually. And everybody else, if they wanted anything they'd look for us to do it. Anything came to them we gave it to them. We gave them what we wanted to give them. Wouldn't nobody mess with us 'cause all those we didn't whup we'd shoot up or maybe even manage to kill. Not too many people said nothing 'cause they was afraid to . . . 'cause we would a had things up tight. It wasn't that we had so much power fighting from hand to hand combat, but the stuff we could promote! We could come down with some hell of a shit! We could come down with the jive.

We had a .22 rifle shoot twenty-six times. We used to tear up more shit coming down through them alleys. We had an old buffalo gun—we had all kinds of jive down there! One time my mother came up and busted me with six shotguns! That stud from the Audy Home was downstairs. I almost got sent to St. Charles. So anyway, we didn't worry about nobody messing with us. They would come down and ask to mess with just one of us, but they had respect for all of us together. And there were a lot of studs in the club at that time, they didn't do anything. That's why they didn't want to say too much 'cause we weren't using the Conservative name. And the Conservative name had started going down. Not even the police would say anything. Only time they would get on our back was when we'd come up the street screaming and hollering, and jump on innocent peoples. But sometimes we did that, and they didn't say anything. They could of been scared themselves. I don't know. And for a while people thought we had actually cut ourselves loose from the group. I guess they thought we was going to cop out.[10]

---

[10] Cop out: in this context, break away from the group.

Now most of the Seniors and Juniors, they didn't have no job . . . at that time. Even Cock Roach. Cock Roach didn't have no job. But we all had jobs. We always stayed clean. Maybe this was something they didn't understand either. They beg most every time we'd see them. And if we didn't have no job, we didn't beg. We go out and get us some money—hit somebody in the head. Steal us something. Like maybe for breakfast when we didn't go home we'd always have a vacant apartment or something like that. One or two of us would go out and steal us some rolls or bacon and eggs, and go up and cook them. On many occasions we did that. It was pretty nice.

We was saying that we going to make the name Mighty Vice Lords go down in history some day. We had so much confidence in ourselves that we felt we could do this here. Actually we was obligated to do it. This was our supreme purpose—to be known, to gain this certain respect. We just wanted to do this.

It was at the meeting, and Count said, "One day the Mighty Vice Lord name will go out to history, and we'll be known nation wide. Everybody will remember the Mighty Vice Lords."

Those were his exact words. And we tried to make it so. We did a little bit of everything up under the sun. People respected us. Every place we went we gained respect. Like one time when we went south. We were out on 63rd, and the peoples knew who we was. And we hadn't mentioned Vice Lords or anything. Everybody respected us to the highest. We were Lords.

See, people respected the Lords in a way 'cause they never run back and say, "Well, this club here jumped on me!" The Lords took care of their own. It was their responsibility to do it. They did it. In a way everybody helped everybody else. We should take care of business if necessary, but we didn't try to boguard[11] nobody and all that—you know, just take things from nobody. When we got it, we got it. It gained us respect and made us welcome anytime we came there. If things got kind of rough, we knew how to take care of the business. But we gained respect for that too.

If you in the Lords, that's one thing. If you's a woman, you'd be a woman. If you's a man, you was a man. That's the way it was. You had to learn. You was out there. You was holding that street twenty-four hours a day. And you just had to constantly fight life and death out there. Lots of times the police even threatened us. Some cat going on about how he was going to shoot us. At that point everybody was against the Lords. We was a little city. That's why they called it Vice Lord City. And you just had to be close or if you wasn't, that was it. You dead. But we had lots of fun together, and that's probably what made us real tight.

The word Vice Lord—it shocked a lot of peoples. It fascinated a lot of peoples. That's probably why lots of the fellows was really digging the club—the Lords. Actually you wasn't nobody, but the word itself mean a lot. You treasure that word. That's why maybe a lot of peoples did what they did. You go through some hell of a changes . . . hell of a changes!! You sit down and talk about it now, and you know, laugh at it. But still one thing that remains bound to you . . . respect. You feel you always deserve respect from any person to you, white or colored. You

---

[11] Boguard: to bully, to "walk over" someone.

learn that. Even our name itself, Mighty Vice Lords, it means something. Mighty in everything. That's right!!

That's one thing about the clubs. I know we went through some hell of a things together, but after it was all over, we didn't care. We all was happy about it. We laughed and drunk our wine. People might talk about it after us, but we was happy. We was the ones that had gained this respect. And I'll tell you one thing about them peoples in the hood. Them peoples wouldn't come up there and tell us to move. You know why? They just as scared of us as we was of them. Actually they had more rights than we did. What could we of gained by it? We couldn't even vote. We didn't have nothing to say.

One thing, it cost us some lots of money as many scrapes as we got in and got out. It cost us some lots of money to get in and get out jail all them times—hell of a lot of money! We spent more money staying out of jail than we did having a good time. That's real, though. That's life. That's no lie, man. That's the way it was.

I shot about six or seven peoples one night. It was kind of funny, though. Little Bull had just got out of jail, and we was down at the YMCA. You know, on Saturday nights we used to go there skating. I'll never forget that. I had just stole a brand new five shot automatic, a J. C. Higgins, and I wanted to test it out.

So one of the fellows run up to me and said, "Go ahead! Here come the Roman Saints!"

So I hid behind the car.

They come marching down there yelling, "We going to tear up these Lords!! We going to do this!! We going to do that!!"

Shit! They come down there, they ain't shit! So anyway, I had it loaded wrong. I didn't know how to load the thing. I squeezed the trigger—and you know how you do, you close your eyes when you getting ready to squeeze the trigger—and didn't nothing happen! So I beat it a little while and rearranged the shell, and put it back up. They was getting closer and closer! Now I wasn't intending to shoot none of them. I was going to shoot the gun and chase them back. Only thing, I wanted to see if the gun was any good. So I squeezed the trigger again, and still didn't nothing happen, man. And this happened three or four times!!!

I was just fixing to say, "This thing ain't no good!! I just as soon throw it away!!" And then I figured maybe I have the safety on.

So I beat it around, played with the safety for a while, and threw the shell up in there again. They was coming, and when they was about fifty feet, they spotted me. You know, before they all run after you they going to congregate a little while. I was backing off. I was scared! But I knew they weren't going to bother me. All I had to do was show the shotgun, and they'd run. So they tried coming forward. I didn't know if the shotgun would even work, man. I was backing up, and they was coming towards me. They all spread out like they were going to come and get me. Yeah! They thought they going to have a party that night!! All of a sudden I squeezed that trigger, and that thing started going off. I had it loaded top! I was just going to shoot one time, but it started so pretty, I said, "Forget it!" Things started going fast, man!! I shot four of them. That barrel was almost melting. You know with an automatic you can't just continue to shoot the gun like that—especially a big gun like that. The gun almost melted on me. The thing was hot. I went and stuck it in some water, man.

Little Bull was with me that night. We hid the gun up under a car. He had a twelve gauge, and I had an automatic. Only thing, he didn't get a chance to shoot his because I was gone so fast. See, that's why I wasn't so worried about them coming after me. Altogether I guess I shot about six or seven of them. That was when Gradman had just came into the court. All the fellows was talking about that new judge. I got fourteen continuances. They shouldn't have even picked me up 'cause they didn't find no shotgun on me. They found the shotgun around the corner.

But what happened, I'm like a fool!! They picked up Little Bull, and I don't know what he said.

One of my partners said, "Well, do you want to go down there and see him?"

I said, "What the fuck, they ain't got nothing on me. I'll go down there with him."

I got down there, and they locked me up! I stayed there until the end of the case. Three of the Saints came down there and identified me. They said I shot them. They never appeared in court. It was at the end of the six month period for that fool Pachek to change courts, and Gradman had just came in . . . after this.

It's funny, I'll never forget this. He said, "You want to go home son?"

At two thirty, man!!

I said, "Yeah!!!"

He said, "Well, go ahead." He said to my mother, "Take him home, ma'am."

I never even looked back! I kept on going!

You'll catch a fool in every crowd, and the Lawndale area is full of fools. Everybody think they know more than everybody else. Nobody know anything . . . no more than somebody else tell them what they might see, or what somebody might hear from their next door neighbor.

And talking about cash, all them fellows working for that Commission on Youth Welfare, all them cats, man . . . that's the the most sickening sight I ever seen. All them sit back there in their office making five to ten thousand dollars a year, running out program after program. They have interviews about what they're doing for the Lawndale area, and one of the biggest well known gangbangers can walk up on them . . . they wouldn't even know who he is. We are strangers to them, but still they going to write, Cupid did this here, or Bull did this here, or Little Lord did this here. I might walk up on them, and they wouldn't know me, Bull walk up on them, they wouldn't know him, Little Lord might walk up on them, they wouldn't know him neither .. . until somebody do something, and then there's a whole lot of bullshit. They shaking hands. Then they want to find jobs for everybody. But as far as them coming out to the streets and want to work on their own, they not going to do that. They don't see no reason why they should do it. It's no use to them. So long as they draw their check it's mellow. When they check stop coming to them, they got to work then. All this is just a thing—a way to make a living. As long as we out on the street and fighting, they got money coming in. But if we want to settle down and just be somebody, they won't accept it then. They say we all savages. But it's not so. Everybody wants to live decent. We not going to be young savages all our life. One day we going to have to be able to vote, and them guys going to be out of a job!

The younger generation coming up, I'm quite sure that they don't want to come up the same way we did. Especially when we get to be part of society, some of those kids going to be ours, and we don't want them going through that same shit we went through—trying to come up being somebody instead of nobody. I guess that's just the way it is. We nobody.

That Youth Commission and all them cats . . . full of shit. Just like they never been. Who know them? Nobody. Who care to know them? Nobody. What they ever did for somebody? Nothing . . . nothing at all. They might interview a couple of peoples when they job's on the line, but come down to cold facts, who they think about? Nobody but themselves. They pass some old exam for this job, so the State decides to give it to them. They living the life of a king. What they got to do? Nothing. What makes their job so easy, the papers do most of they work. All they have to do is hop up and read the papers, ask a couple of questions, and write a report. They might not send it in for six months. That's it. But for them to get down to real problems . . . no good. What I believe the caseworkers should do if they was really out for the peoples is to be really true to they work. But you can't be a true caseworker with so many peoples who all got problems. Like in Lawndale, how many caseworkers do they got? About fifty. Now how in the hell can fifty caseworkers take care of damn near four or five thousand boys, all who got problems?! Half of them ain't got clothes to wear to school, and nowhere to get any from. Half of them are drop-outs, and ain't nobody trying to get no job for them. And out of that fifty caseworkers, maybe about ten is looking out for their job—they're looking out for the fellows—and the other forty just there. They might as well not be there —just a lot of expense, just a way to spend money. It's sickening!

I got on parole that time I shot my father, I was mad at somebody else. I had a .32 revolver, and I was going to shoot Gowster Dan and Pork Chop. They were talking this old simple stuff. I don't even remember what they talking about now.

So I was coming out the room, and my father said, "Where you going?"

I said, "I'm going out."

He was trying to stop me. He must have felt I had a gun 'cause he right there. So we got to arguing.

I said, "Get away from the door!"

He said, "What you going to do?"

"If you don't get away from the door, I'm going to leave you laying there and go out the back way! It don't make me no difference!"

He kept arguing, so I threw out my jive. My mother attracted my attention, and he went on downstairs and called the police. But he was going to drop the charges. They tricked him into signing the complaint. They said he had to sign, and this is not true.

That fool Pachek gave me a year probation. He gave me the first sixty days in the Joint,[12] and a year's probation. But it was about the first good thing he ever did. Lucky he didn't say a year in the Joint. He was pretty good at that.

He said, "well . . . a . . . did you point the gun at your father?"

You know, that little gleam he had in his eye? He just waiting to send me away. I looked at that little gleam, and I thought. I knew what I better not say.

I said, "I ain't going to start pointing a gun at my father!"

I started to say it was a play gun. He never would have knowed it. But one thing messed me up. See, like a fool I went and showed them where I put that gun at. I shouldn't have showed them that. If I hadn't shown them, it'd just been my word against my father's. I could have told them it was a toy gun or something then.

I met Venus at a dance. Me and Count was together, and it was on a Friday night. I'll never forget it! Count'd just got off work, and we went down to his crib. He was living on Douglas and Drake. When we left, we went around to this girl's house I used to go with. We stayed up there maybe five or ten minutes—no later than fifteen. We rapped[13] for awhile, and then Count said he was going to this dance.

So I told him, "O.K., I meet you there," and he cut out. So I said, "Well, I don't think I'm going." I told her I had changed my mind, and I'd better go on home and go to bed.

So I cuts out down 16th street, and I meets some more of the fellows. Pork Chop was there. They was talking about this dance, so while I was there I thought I might as well go on up there. And then's when I met Venus.

When I first seen her I thought I knew her. So I was talking to her. I was just talking to her as a friend—just trying to get acquainted. I think things got a little bit out of hand though, afterwards. We didn't do anything, but I just started seeing her more often.

O.K., she told me she was pregnant. Well to me, somebody give me their word about something like that, I'm not going to act like a fool and question them —knowing I had something to do with them.

I'm not going to say, "Well . . . is you sure?"

I'm figuring you should know, 'cause you supposed to be a woman. I take care my part of the business, you take care of yours. Well, it come out a couple of months later she wasn't pregnant. Then it come out that she was pregnant. I didn't know what the hell to believe! And it come out this time, she was pregnant for real. Finally we just gone on and got married. I wish I hadn't.

But see, since she said she was pregnant, I'm not the type of fellow to say, "Well . . . a . . . it's not my baby! It could be anybody's baby!" like some people say.

I kind of liked the girl anyway. I knew eventually I'd get attached to her, and the baby means a lots anyway. So I asked her to marry me, and she said O.K.

It was going all right. We lived on 18th and Springfield. It was all right for

---

[12] The Joint: the House of Correction, in jail.
[13] Rapped: talked.

the first week or two. Then she got this urge that she continuous wanted to go over to her mother's house. She spend more time in her mother's house than she did with me. Everytime we get in an argument she running back to her mother. So I asked her what's over to her mother's house?

She said, "I can't go over to visit my mother?"

I said, "It's O.K. to visit your mother, but why visit her every week? I don't even visit my mother every week, and she lives just about three blocks from me!"

But it don't stop. She continually running back and forth. Then her partner, she came over and talked her into going to Michigan. Which I didn't know nothing about. On Thursday she come to me and tells me she going to Michigan.

I said, "Going to Michigan? Well, you didn't ask me nothing about it!"

"If you don't want me to go, I won't go."

So I went to work, and when I came home she had borrowed some money from the landlord and went to Michigan. She came back that Monday, and we got into it. She talking about killing herself. I believe she some kind of nut! Something wrong with the girl, actually something wrong with her. So she went over to her mother's house, and I went to work. When I came home there she was. But it didn't stop. She continuous going back and forth to her mother's house. On the Fourth of July, that was the last argument we had. She said she was going to her mama's to stay. So I stayed that night, and the next day I wrapped my clothes and left. She came back looking for me saying about how she planning to come back home, but I said no good. It wasn't the point that I had got tired of her, I had just got tired of her running back and forth to her mother. Her mother wasn't meaning us no good noways. I figured if she wanted to stay with her mother, she should have stayed with her mother before we got married. And I was still a nice enough guy that after I had found she had lied to me about being pregnant, I still didn't say anything about it. I could have just went on and ended things right then, and it would have been lots more simpler than it is now.

See, I'm trying to make something. I'm not getting no younger, and I want to at least have something before I get forty or fifty years old and can't do anything. What can you do when you forty or fifty? You can live, but that's all. I want to work maybe fifteen or twenty years 'til I'm thirty-five, maybe forty, and have me something saved up. Good! Then I could kind of slack down and live as I want to live. But right now it'd look kind of foolish everytime I save up fifty dollars, go out and spend it . . . for nothing, and come back and have to work twice as hard trying to do something else. But she don't seem to understand that. As soon as she get a dollar she want to run and spend it. She just didn't never growed up, but she actually figure that she's the only person that grown up. She figure that I'm still a boy and she a woman. She just don't understand. She figure she just more grown up than I am. It's generally like that 'cause I felt the same way when I was on the streets—that I was more grown up than anybody on the streets. I would always tell somebody else something, but couldn't nobody tell me anything.

And quite naturally she couldn't have been on the streets that long and got a baby. Anybody know that! Look at these girls on the streets. Look at these Vice Ladies and Cobraettes. You know, they been through all kinds of hell, and ain't none . . . very few of them girls out there got babies. They're prostitutes and everything else, and ain't none of them got no babies. They move away, and they be just like anybody else when don't nobody know them. Then you take these fools that come in and ain't been no place and don't know nothing, and try to tell you something. Sure, I listen . . . and some things she say make sense—you know, make you feel sorry for her, but the point is, I can learn something from her, and I been out there with them kinds of peoples. Seems like she should learn a little more than I'm learning, and she ain't been out there with them. But she just don't see it like that.

Like now, she on the ADC, and she going to school. The ADC don't know she's going. I'm paying $100 a month for support, and she paying out pretty close to sixty dollars a month going to school. What the hell's the baby getting?! The baby's going to have to eat!

It's actually funny—her trying to be slick. If I don't pay, it'd be cheaper for me to go to jail. They not going to keep me no more than thirty days or sixty at the most. They can't keep me forever for not giving somebody something that's not theirs—that's be mine. I'm obligated to pay some, but why all this when I'm not even with her. I'll pay for something that's mine, but not for something that's not mine.

And she's just steady going to school. Sure, I could understand if she was going to school at night. Let her go at night. She don't have to pay nobody. If I'm going to give her twenty-five dollars a week, let me watch the kids. Don't give my money to somebody else while you go to school during the daytime, and the kid's half getting mistreated. And you still got them ADC peoples on my back about that support. You not doing right yourself. Making me look like a fool. I have to work twice as hard, and can't even get a decent place to live. And then she just throwing away money.

What she doing going back to school? She be twenty years old, and in 3A. Kind of silly. Stupid! When you have a baby, and the baby ain't but three months old, you not well. You can't get up at no six o'clock in the morning every morning —talking about going to school—and get back at three-thirty. And . . . you can't keep a house. You know, you're tired enough as is just having the baby. Trying to do like everybody else—running around that school, running up and down stairs. You going to run around with your friends. Weekends you going to try and go out. You going to stay up to about ten—twelve o'clock. So how in the hell can you do all that? And at night the baby going to wake up too. All through the night you going to give him his bottle. That's a whole lot of jive. It's tough. It's hard enough just keeping the baby. And there he is, he got diaper rash 'cause she too lazy to get up and dry him. She supposed to find a baby sitter to keep my baby! She getting better now, though, since I went up side her head.

How long she going to be able to go to school if that baby get sick one time? She fool around, she send herself to jail. O.K., she don't take that baby to the clinic like he supposed to be taken, and the baby fool around and die, she going to be into it. She can't look at me and say I didn't do my part even though I didn't give her the money. She's supposed to be the mother. That's her part. Anytime the mother don't care about her own child, you know damn well what the father think. She the one that went through all them pains. Like I say, I care for my child, but the mother . . . see, the mother supposed to have a little more respect for the kids than I supposed to have. If something go wrong, it makes me kind of think if she don't give a damn, why should I? She let her sister wash and feed my baby, and her sister about ten—eleven years old. What do a girl ten or eleven look like washing a baby? If some mothers can wash and keep their babies in order, why can't she? It's kind of funny.

And to show how stupid she was, she called herself getting money from the ADC peoples. They'd sent it when they felt like it. At least I was stopping by and giving her ten or fifteen dollars when she was asking for it. But she steady asking for more and more money. How the hell I'm going to give her more money? O.K., I wouldn't mind giving her five dollars, and then giving her another five dollars if she going to take care of the first five dollars. If she won't take care of the first five dollars it's kind of hard to give her another five dollars.

And our problem, see, she liked to ask me for money and didn't want me to ask what she going to do with it. Who the hell's going to give somebody some money unless they know what they're going to do with it? If I walked up and said, "Give me fifteen dollars" you going to ask me what I'm going to do with it.

She ask me, "Well, give me fifteen dollars?"

I say, "What you going to do with it?"

She say, "There you go again! Everytime I ask you for some money, you all ask me what I'm going to do with it."

Why the hell should I give her some of my money?! I worked all week for it, and she sit up there on ADC, and she don't give me nothing when I ask for it. She just making it for herself. Her rent cost seventy-five dollars a month, and she isn't getting but a hundred and twenty-nine dollars a month. She just barely making it. And now she won't even have a holiday steak. And see, my first chance to leave, I'm going to leave. What kind of fool's going to go around paying that kind of money?

Actually the Aid is not for her anyway. They mostly give you that money for your kids. You get a certain something, but you don't get as much as your kids . . . I imagine. You get enough 'cause you supposed to be their guardian, or something like that. And it's not actually your house. Anytime somebody comes to your house anytime they want to and look around, and you can't have who you want there, and you can't have no telephone, you can't have a this, can't have a television. Who the hell want to live like that? They're doing this and they think they slick! How in the hell you slick? You ain't slick! You a stone fool! If you going to get a hundred and twenty-nine dollars a month, you better off working for it than somebody giving it to you! Anytime somebody give you something, they always want something for it. But she thinks she doing right, she actually think she doing right. She just don't know. Anytime you ready for somebody to give you something before you ready to work for something, you in bad shape. That's one thing we always did when I was on the streets. If we couldn't take it from nobody, don't give it to us. We didn't want it . . . 'cause there's going to be something behind it. Somebody'd always end up getting hurt behind it, or something. Always like that. You give us two dollars, tomorrow you going to want four or five. Now anytime you act like you got it, we'll take it from you, but don't just walk up and say, "Here's two dollars. Buy yourself something to drink." Nope, we don't go for it.

I always felt that I was capable of taking care of myself. If I wanted something, I knew how to get it . . . one way or another. And I always felt can't that man help me if I can't help myself. That's the way I still feel about things. If I can't make my own decisions, can't nobody make them for me. I know right from wrong if I want to do it. The right way for me to do it is my way . . . the way I want to go. If I don't want to go, I'm not going to do it. I don't care who make the laws and who don't make the laws. It's my decision what I want to do. If I want to do it, I'm going to do it. Nothing wrong with that. It's common sense, you know. I feel this way. The law is there. It's something that people made. I mean, everybody know right from wrong, man. Law is for the fools. People like . . . I feel this here. Peoples say we not civilized. Well, I'll bet you tomorrow morning you'll find more of them peoples in jail than you'll find of us . . . for beating their wife. If they're not beating their wife, they're in there for disorderly conduct—drunk and disorderly—or something. Now we did gang fight, but we did it for a purpose. What's their purpose in doing it? We young, but they thirty-five or forty years old. But still when they read the paper about us they say, "It's a shame! Those young hoodlums, those young punks . . . they need to be put away!" But they forget a week before that they was in jail for disorderly conduct. Shit!

I knew there was a certain restriction in the laws about what we could do, but I feel this way. In certain cases we just stretched the laws a little bit more . . . you know, than the way they should of been stretched. But at the time we *did* do this . . . What's did is did. At that time I figured it was the right thing for me to do and I did it. It's one of them things like anything else. I'm not ashamed I did it. Once I start being ashamed of something I did I'll be just like everybody else—no confidence in myself. I'll never amount to anything. I'll always be scared to make a decision. I don't want to ever be that way. Maybe the decision is wrong. If it's wrong, if it comes up again I'll know not to do it.

When you on the streets you learn what's what. That's something they don't teach you in school. School don't teach you about life. It teaches you about past life —what somebody had did, and how somebody made something. It don't teach you about how to live. And this is something they can't teach you . . . unless you be in the streets. School put education in you head, but the streets tell you what you going to do when you grown. The streets teach you how to live.

O.K., say a stud got a education. Oh yeah, he give you the right answer for what's two and two, but he couldn't go out in the street and make five dollars like you could . . . or couldn't tell you what's happening. Education, it does mean something, though. You might get a job before me. But the peoples that actually know what they doing, the peoples that're making it . . . what I mean is you can't really make it unless you know what's happening in the streets. I don't care how much education you got, if you don't know how to live in the streets, it don't mean nothing. A fellow like me, I figure well at least I know I'm living in the streets. Anytime I'm out in the streets I can make myself a hustle. You dig? I always can make myself a buck . . . if I want to bad enough. 'Cause there's always somebody on the street, a fool. There's always a fool out there! I don't care what generation you is, you always going to find a fool. And every time the price go up—every time a more intelligent fool come out in the street, then you got to be a little bit more intelligent.

And maybe those people in school be more advanced than me, but on the long run you got to look at this here. The thing will equal up because in order for them to use this knowledge, they got to first come on the street. And half those people with all that education haven't got the stomach to live on the street and go through all that shit. And because their parents put them in school so young, they don't know the first thing about the streets, so they might fall ten or twelve years behind me. While they're trying to learn how to live on the streets, I'll catch up with them. That's where my parents upped theirs . . . 'cause I know whats going on. I know what's out there. They don't know what is what—what's happening. They don't know nothing about nothing. And as much as nine out of ten times they'll get lost . . . or end up a gangster.

What you learn on the streets is how to live. See, you never know who might knock on your door. Like I say, I might hit you in the head and rob you tonight, and tomorrow I wouldn't know who I hit. Half the time you don't care. I might not remember your face but you might remember mine . . . so you got to be very observant. You learn to do certain things. You learn your senses. You learn to smell things, you learn to control your ways. Out south, out north, or out west there's a whole lot of gangbangers whereever you go. Like out south there're the Rangers, out north the Continental Pimps, and out west there're the Vice Lords and Cobras too. That why I say at least all of them been on the streets and they know what's happening. All them people with that education, they don't even know what's happening.

I could tell them some things they don't know about too—how to get along with peoples. I could get along with some peoples they couldn't. There's certain things I could understand about them peoples that they couldn't. Take the caseworkers. They're all short tempered because they don't have the patience to stake out to what their ideas would be about life. They won't take the time out to see how they feel about what is what. And all them caseworkers are always telling, telling! How the hell can you tell somebody something? I can't tell you, or anybody what to do. I can maybe make a suggestion about how you might better yourself about this and that. But life's a funny thing, that's all I can do.

Now I'm not old. I'm in what you call the middle grade. I'm out of my teens. I'm twenty years old, and the five out of the twenty I was out there in the street I learned more than in all the other fifteen . . . because of the different people I run into, and the incidents that happened. Actually I learned how to find myself, how to look up and face responsibility—things that everybody didn't give you. It was always this way in a club. There's somebody always depending on you. Somebody always looking up to you to do something so they could keep on going. This gives you a good feeling. So you do it, and they do it. But everybody in a club got to change and go through a different way of life. You not going to be a gangfighter all your life. People steady advertising you need this, you need that. You need doctors, you need lawyers, undertakers, and you think what you're losing. So you got to change.

Don't care what anybody says, we don't mean no harm to nobody if they don't mess with us. See, we respect some older people than us. As long as they don't mess with us, we don't mess with them. Yeah, just like Wyatt Earp. See, Wyatt Earp was supposed to be a law abiding man. If anybody messed up, they seen Wyatt Earp. But if you didn't mess up, you didn't see Wyatt. The same way with us. And you know what people said?

They said, "If you don't mess with them Vice Lords, Vice Lords won't mess with you."

Same way with Wyatt Earp and his town. And this's why the Vice Lords begin to have a city. And then pretty soon they said we had an organization. But all we thought, we just buddy-buddy. See, some people think the wrong way. They think the Vice Lord's just trying to be bad—build up a reputation. But we don't think that way. We not only just building our rep. We laying back drinking wine having a good time for the time being until we can get a job. See, we don't want to be laying on the street all the time. This is the point that the public don't see. They figure that we some kind of cattle. Once you be branded, you can't take the brand off of you. They figure that just because you might have a record, or a reputation, it's all over. But this is something that nobody seems to understand—what you did in your younger days is not something you can't grow out of. Everybody has to grow up. And now the way they acting, they acting just like we was in our younger days. Like they not letting us face responsibilities—the public, the people, the welfare. Now you can't blame all the welfare. It's some of our fault, some of their fault. It's a hell of a thing.

Look, there's twenty-eight thousand people living in the Robert Taylor housing project. How many more living in Lawndale area? And count the centers, or the playgrounds. Can't everybody get a basketball . . . not too many places you can get a baseball. And in the Lawndale area, how many people's on the welfare so they can't afford to buy this stuff? And in the area how many people go to school . . . if they ain't kicked out? How many don't have the self-confidence in not having the clothes and the money to go to school? Some peoples say a dollar's not a lot, but how many peoples got a dollar to pay for a book? How many people got thirteen cents to catch the bus every day? There's a lot more to it than people see. But people not trying to see. Only thing people see is young savages.

All they say is, "They savages! They don't need a chance!"

There's two sides to every story. They not looking at it that way though. To me they're just more savage to me than I am to them. We both live in two complete different worlds. Actually I'll probably make it to the top before they will because at least I got something to fight for. I want to be independent. They don't.

They going to look at the next person, and the next person going to say, "I think those boys need to be put away."

Then this person going to say, "I think you right! They should be put away. Them boys shouldn't have no place in this society. None at all!"

That's what they saying. "They young savages! Throw them away! Put them in jail!"

But they don't need to be on the street. They don't know the first thing about it. Half of these peoples out here don't even know who the President is today, and they got nerve enough to talk about what is what. It's the truth! Half these people don't even know what this Viet Nam problem is about, and they supposed to be citizens. And most of these peoples out here don't know who in the hell they voting for. That's true. Everybody know that. That's how Walker got in Congress. He's the biggest hypocrite I ever seen.

Everybody say, "He's the most generous, most kindest man I ever seen."

He don't do nothing but sit around and give his flunkies mail to mail. Walker's a smart man. I give it to him in this case 'cause he can fool the ignorant person. They come in after a hard day's work and not interested in nothing.

They say, "Well, I think Walker's a smart man. Let's vote for Walker."

Will Walker build them a couple of hospitals? No! Will Walker cut down taxes a half a cent? No! Walker *in* next year. If you're making fifty dollars a week, if taxes raised a half a cent you going to lose that month. Walker's your man! You put him in office. Fuck Walker! To me frontier days better than it is now. At least everybody wore a gun. You didn't have to pay nobody to shoot you down. You know what to expect then. But now, it's a hell of a thing. You out doing something, and you steady paying taxes, and the police, the man you paying, comes up and shoots you in the head, or shoots you in the back. It's a hell of a thing.

The average fellow in a club is not stupid. They can't be stupid and be in a club, facing danger everyday. This is something the government itself train you for —how to stay alive. This is why they draft peoples into the army. But ourselves, we didn't need it. You can't lecture to us about it 'cause if we didn't do it, we'd die, get killed. We learned how to fight, how to help yourself to something. Like if you needed money or something, you know how to get it . . . if you didn't want to work for it. And half the time we didn't want to work 'cause we didn't see why we should work when people steady dominating us anyway. People gave us the name of being savages so we just *be* savages. But we still feel we a little bit better than they are.

I'm out the Lords. I just got tired of fighting so I got out. You know, you don't stay in a club. Anytime a fellow join a club he grabbing for something. Everybody join a club reaching for a certain goal, and when you reach that goal, that's it. Like maybe you're reaching for something. When you reach for that, when you get it, you're going to start reaching for something else, you know. It's a steady thing. I joined the Lords to gain respect and get known—across the neighborhood. And I gained it . . . in a way—some ways good, and some ways bad because in the way I gained it I did develop more enemies than I did friends. Maybe the first time I turn my back somebody might run up on me. I don't know. All I can say, when you're out there you don't know who's sisters and brothers. You shoot . . . and it could be some of your own peoples. You don't know nothing about that. You know, there's people in you family you don't know, and on occasions you might be fighting them.

So I just got out, that's all. But just because you get out of a club, you still owes certain . . . you don't really owe anything, but you feel . . . like they come around and they ask you for something to drink or something, I mean, you feel that this is only something that you should give it to them. But going out and gangbanging with them, that's no good. I wouldn't even hang around with them much 'cause it shows a certain kind of something. People look at it as you still there. And when you hanging with a group . . . peoples is peoples. Peoples don't understand why you hang with them, who you are, or what. Peoples name you. Peoples name the club. Yeah! That's how peoples react if you're a teenager. Once you a Lord, you branded for the rest of your life.

R. Lincoln Keiser.

7

Fieldwork Among the Vice Lords

Editorial Introduction

In the chapter following Lincoln Keiser shows how the urban ghetto situation and racism affected his field research. These pervasive factors are apparent in his getting introduced to the leadership of the Vice Lords, establishing residence in the ghetto, gaining entrée to the fighting club, and in the special problems of participant observation in the organization. In the ghetto environment, a White among Blacks, his role was complex. Although he got on the inside, he remained an outsider and racism in some form was always present as a barrier even with his best friends. That he and his friends among the Vice Lords surmounted this barrier sufficiently to permit the research to be done at all, is an indication that this barrier need not prevent some degree of effective mutual understanding.

He also deals with the influence of his own theoretical orientation on his fieldwork, showing how it was a factor determining what he observed, how he asked questions, and how he interpreted what he saw and heard.

G. D. S.

Introduction

For some time many anthropologists and sociologists have felt that the particular research techniques developed through the study of small-scale societies had limited, if any, value for research in modern industrial urban communities. Michael Banton has said, for example, "The relatively simple life of a tribal village can perhaps be adequately described in purely verbal terms but the uniformities found in urban life can for the most part be expressed only statistically. In the town few generalizations of any validity can be obtained without

In Vice Lord territory.

the use of social survey techniques . . ." (1957: xv). Sociologists have expressed similar views concerning the use of anthropological methods in studying urban phenomena. "When studying an entire primitive society in this way [using anthropological methods] one can be fairly certain of having witnessed the full range of behavior that members of that society hold in high regard, given the relatively constant constraints of the physical environment. However, when this method is applied to subcultures contained within a single society, it is apt to lead to fallacious results . . ." (Short and Strodtbeck 1965:75).

Recently, however, a significant number of anthropologists have begun to go into the city, and have taken with them basic ways of studying human behavior that were developed through the analysis of peasant and tribal groups. But cities are quite different from the kinds of places where anthropologists have traditionally worked, and this difference generates different problems, both of a practical and theoretical kind. In this chapter I will explore some of the problems that I encountered and the ways I tried to solve them in my research with the Vice Lords, a Black street gang located in the Lawndale area of Chicago's West Side ghetto. I shall discuss problems that derive from approaching the study of human behavior from a particular anthropological orientation, as well as problems that are related to the particular nature of cities.

There is another important factor that is not directly related to the urban setting as such. This derives from the racial situation in the United States. I was a White working in a Black ghetto area, and this had definite effects on my research. Some of these effects will be discussed in this chapter.

There are certain kinds of problems that almost all anthropologists face when undertaking any piece of field research. It will be helpful here to enumerate some of these briefly. Later in the chapter each will be discussed in terms specific to my research. In undertaking a field research project, one must first pick out an area in which to do research and choose what will be studied. Then there is the problem of getting established. This involves settling physically in the area; becoming adjusted to living in an alien environment; and establishing the necessary social relationships so that one can begin gathering data. Data gathering itself presents problems. On one level this involves data-gathering techniques, but on another level there is the problem of what, out of the almost infinite array of human behavioral aspects, one chooses to record in the first place. Although the latter is related to the explicit purposes the researcher has in undertaking the study, it is also related to the anthropologist's basic theoretical orientation, for this generates ideas concerning what is problematical in human behavior, and, therefore, what is to be recorded. The anthropologist is not always conscious of this orientation while he is actively involved in field research, and thus he is not always aware of how it is affecting what he records. The anthropologist's emotional reactions to the social and cultural setting in which he is working is another source of problems. Having to interact in social situations where one does not know the cultural significance of various actions places a tremendous emotional strain on the individual, and affects his relationships with the people he is studying. Also, although the anthropologist tries to approach his work as dispassionately as possible, he is a human being, and he reacts to situations in terms of his own values and ideas. How the anthropologist handles these feelings is one of the most serious problems of field research. Finally, after the research has been completed, there is the problem of writing up the material into some kind of coherent account.

Picking an Area and Topic

The choice of an area and a research topic can be made in several ways. One may be primarily interested in a particular geographic area and then develop a research topic appropriate to that area. In other cases one's primary interest may lie in a particular topic, say for example, political anthropology, and the geographic area is chosen for its special relevance to the topical interest. In both these situations, however, the choice of one's first fieldwork project usually stems from reading and other work done in the course of undergraduate and graduate training.

My choice of a Black gang (or "club," as it is known in the ghetto) for a research topic came about a little differently. In 1963, while I was a graduate student at Northwestern University, I had a part time job as a waiter in the dining room of a luxurious retirement home located in Evanston, a suburb of Chicago. Blacks were hired as kitchen help by the company who ran the dining room, while Whites did the work that involved contact with the patrons. Most of the Black workers were women, but there were a few men my age who worked as dishwashers. Part of my job consisted of clearing the tables after a meal and taking the dirty dishes to the counter in front of the dishwasher. Thus I got to know Jesse and Al, the two dishwashers. We never became really close friends, but I did get to know them well enough so that my presence did not interrupt their normal conversation. Often I would sit with them during a break, and linger at the dishwasher to exchange a few words. Al had grown up in a neighborhood in Chicago that had no fighting clubs. He had met a girl in a bar, and wanted to see her again. But she lived in the neighborhood of a subgroup of the Egyptian Cobras. Jesse was from that neighborhood, had been a member of the Cobras, and knew that this girl was considered by the Cobras to be the "old lady" of one of the group's important members. He considered it his duty to "run it down" (explain it) to Al. Thus the Cobras were a constant conversation topic. I heard bits and snatches of the conversation—enough to be aware that here, in the world of the fighting clubs, was a highly interesting cultural and social system in operation.

My interest was aroused because I was involved in anthropology and reading about how cultural and social systems worked, but my initial contact with the world of the fighting clubs had nothing to do with my anthropological background. My initial contact was primarily related to two factors—the nature of cities, and the operation of racism in the United States. Cities are, among other things, huge conglomerates of people, few of whom know one another. In small-scale societies, those in close spatial proximity usually have many kinds of social interrelationships, for example, kinship relationships, economic relationships, and political relationships. Another way of putting this is that in small-scale societies there are few, if any, strangers. Everyone knows everyone else, and knows them in a variety of social contexts. There are lines of potential social interaction laid out at birth among almost everyone, and individuals activate these at particular times. This is not the case in the city. Many people who are in close spatial proximity have no social relationships, for example, passengers on a bus or subway car. Others who do have social relationships have highly contextualized ones, that is, they relate to one another in a single, or at best, a few contexts only. An individual may relate to one set of people at his job, another set in his home, and yet another set in his club. In the city the process of laying out lines of potential social interaction has an importance lacking in small-scale societies. Another way of putting this is that in the city most people are strangers, and making friends out of strangers is an important and continual social process. Friends are made out of strangers through the interaction that takes place in particular social contexts. For example, a person gets to know others by interacting with them in his job, or at his church, or at parties, or in the classroom. My initial contact with Black fighting clubs was a result of a process of making friends out of strangers that is an integral part of urban social systems.

It is here that racism became important. My initial contact with the world of Black fighting gangs resulted from establishing social relationships with individuals who were a part of this world. That this occurred in the context of a job is related to racism. There were no gang members in any of my anthropology classes at Northwestern; there were no gang members at any of the student parties I attended. In our society at the time I met Jesse and Al, Whites who formed relationships with Blacks, usually, although not always, did so in the context of a job. Middle-class Whites who formed relationships with lower-class Blacks, almost always formed them in the job context. Racism limited the kinds of jobs open to Blacks, and thus limited the kinds of jobs in which I could have met and gotten to know ghetto-dwelling Blacks. Working as a low-paid dishwasher was a job poorly educated Black men could get. If Al and Jesse could have gotten better jobs, quite possibly I never would have met them, and never have made contact with the world of Black fighting clubs.

My job at the retirement home ended, and I lost contact with Jesse and Al. By then I had become interested in fighting clubs. I now knew that certain fighting clubs were not composed of a small number of young men as I had originally thought, but had quite large memberships which were internally organized in complex ways. I had heard references made to Juniors, Seniors, and Midgets; to K-Town Cobras, Jew-Town Cobras, and King Cobras; and to war counselors, supreme war couselors, and presidents. I had heard it said that people had "heart" and "reps." How did this all work? What was the nature of the subgroups? How were they differentiated, and how did they connect with one another? What were the social identities, and how were they connected to form social roles? What were the beliefs, concepts, and values which the members of the clubs held, and how did they fit with the set of social groups and social identities? In short, the question that came to my mind was, what is the nature of this social and cultural system and how does it work? I felt that indeed, here was an area well worth future research.

Getting Established

The next problem was getting established, that is, establishing relationships with members of a particular group; settling in some kind of residence; and adjusting to living in a different environment. Establishing relationships was difficult. No one, much less a White, can go into an area inhabited by a club and initiate a research project. Very careful and time-consuming ground work has to be done. It is necessary to make contact with influential members of the group and to gain their trust before one can begin serious work. I approached this problem again through the means of a job. I was offered employment with the Social Service Department of what was then the Municipal Court of Chicago, and was assigned as a court caseworker to Boys' Court North. Boys' Court North handled cases of boys seventeen through twenty years old. Its spatial jurisdiction included the Lawndale area of Chicago's west side Black ghetto, and the court dealt with members of three large fighting clubs—the Egyptian Cobras, the Roman Saints, and the Vice Lords. The court caseworker's job consisted of counseling individuals referred by the court; thus I became acquainted with members of these three groups.

The Social Service Department was interested in learning about the nature of fighting clubs, and I was given permission to question persons referred to me by the court about features of club life. This posed problems. My role as caseworker conflicted in some ways with my role as anthropologist. As a caseworker my primary purpose was to help the people referred to me make the kind of adjustment to the urban world that would prevent their coming into conflict with the rules and enforcement agencies of predominantly White, middle-class Chicago. This meant I was trying to change behavior in terms of my own value system. As an anthropologist, however, it was crucial to try not to judge behavior relative to my own values, much less to change it. Since my primary responsibility was to the role of caseworker, I was seriously limited in the use of my "clients" as anthropological informants. Further, because I was connected with the court, many boys were reticent to give information about their club. In spite of these difficulties, I was able to gather some basic material. The people most willing to talk about their group were Vice Lords, and, therefore, most of my information was about that club.

In order to conduct further research, I had to establish relationships outside the court context. I accomplished this, however, through my involvement with the court. While talking with a "client" referred by the court, I was told about a woman who had taught in a West Side school, and who had become close friends with several Vice Lords. I contacted her, and she agreed to introduce me to Sonny, one of the Vice Lords she knew. At the time I met Sonny, I also met another Lord called Goliath. In the next year Sonny, Goliath, and I went to parties together, met in bars, and visited each other's homes. During this time I also met a few other members of the club and collected several life histories. It happened that Goliath and I got along especially well, and in the course of the year became quite good friends. In the fall of 1965 I returned to graduate school, and in the summer of 1966 initiated full-scale research.

At the beginning of the summer I approached Goliath with my plan. I would rent an apartment in the ghetto, and Goliath would live with me rent free. In return he would introduce me to the leaders of the Vice Lords, and give assurance that I was not a police spy. Goliath agreed, and the plan was initiated.

Finding an apartment proved more difficult than I had anticipated. Most of the apartments in Lawndale are owned by White absentee landlords, and they were highly suspicious of my motives for wanting to live in the ghetto. When I went to see about renting one apartment, the landlord said, "I'm sorry, we only rent to Whites." I looked at him and said, "Well . . .?" He gave me an embarrassed laugh and said, "Oh, I mean Negroes." Goliath ruled out other available apartments because they afforded too much opportunity for ambush attacks. Finally, after we were unable to find anything suitable in the area around 15th Street, we looked in the North Side ghetto, and found an apartment there. It would have been best to live within the 15th Street Lord's territory. But on the north side I was at least located in a Black neighborhood; I was able to question informants in surroundings that were relatively natural for them; and I was able to give "sets" (parties) for the Vice Lords that were not only useful in gaining rapport, but which also gave me an opportunity to observe behavior in this important social context.

At the beginning of the summer Goliath introduced me to Tex, Bat Man, and Shotgun, three of the most important leaders of the 15th Street Vice Lords. The 15th Street Lords was a section of the City Lords (see Keiser 1969 for a discussion of Vice Lord sections and branches), and I concentrated my research for the first half of the summer on 15th Street. About halfway through the summer Tex was arrested for strong armed robbery, and sentenced to prison. At about the same time, many of the older Vice Lords were released from prison and they decided to reorganize the club. Meetings of the "Nation" (the entire club is called the "Conservative Vice Lord Nation"), attended by members of all the subgroups, were reinstituted. Through Goliath I approached these older individuals who had become the leaders of the Nation. I explained that I wanted to write a book about the Vice Lords, and offered to share any royalties with the group. The proposal was put before the club in a meeting, and with the support of my friends in the 15th Street Lords, and some of the people I had known as a caseworker, the majority of members gave their approval. This legitimized my position in the eyes of the other club members, and the rest of the summer I concentrated my research on the corner of 16th and Lawndale, the meeting place for all the Lords in the branch known as Vice Lord City.

Adjusting to living conditions was nowhere near as difficult in my Vice Lord research as it was in my study of a mountain village in Afghanistan where conditions were similar to those usually encountered by anthropologists working in non-Western societies. I lived in an apartment that, although dingy, had hot and cold running water, a bathroom, and a stove and refrigerator; I bought my food in supermarkets and restaurants with money I was accustomed to using; and the language spoken was generally similar to my own. However, there were some differences that took some adjustment on my part. The greatest of these was getting accustomed to living with the possibility of robbery and ambush. Goliath took many precautions in choosing an apartment that had a well-lighted entrance and well-lighted hallways. We kept a .45 pistol in the apartment, along with several wooden clubs. Goliath always put a match in the door jam before we left so that he could tell if anyone had forced open the door while we were gone and might be hidden in the apartment when we came back. At night he put boards and empty cans in front of the windows and doors so that if someone tried to break in, he would make so much noise that we would be awakened. These were precautions that any sensible person took—like buckling your safety belt while driving in an automobile. Goliath no more dwelt on the possibility of someone attacking us, than I dwell on the possibility of being killed in an automobile accident. There are dangers, you take precautions, and go about living a normal life. It took a while for me to get used to taking these precautions without getting extremely nervous. It turned out they saved me possible trouble and injury. Early one morning a man forced his way into our apartment through a window. He knocked over the board we had set up and awakened me. I was waiting for him with a two-by-four (Goliath had spent the night with a girlfriend and had taken the .45 with him), and when he saw me, he turned around and went back out the window.

Gathering the Data

There are two aspects of the problem of gathering data. First, is the problem of methods. The ones I used are standard in anthropological fieldwork: I did participant observation and conducted interviews with informants. For me, participant observation consisted of observing behavior while hanging out on the streets, going to bars, attending parties, visiting friends and relatives, and simply driving about the West Side with members of the club. As a participant observer I was involved in the first stages of one actual gang fight, and was part of the preparations for another that never materialized. My presence in the neighborhood was legitimized by me being "the man who is writing the book." People knew what I was doing there, and why I was doing it. But I could never fully participate in the life of the streets. For one thing, not everyone accepted me to the same extent. For some, the fact that I was White seemed to cause little difficulty. In conversation, Vice Lords often call one another "nigger" in a joking manner. When "nigger" was used in conversation by a person who did not know me very well, often he would turn and say, "Oh, excuse me," as if he had insulted me. One time when this was said, a friend of mine answered, "That don't make no difference, Jack. The man's a nigger just like us, only he's white. He's a white nigger." Others had such strong antagonisms that they were unable to be friends with me. They tolerated my presence, but for the most part ignored me. Finally, there were some individuals who could not control their hatred toward Whites, and in a few instances it boiled into the open aimed at me. When this happened, I simply walked away.

But to an extent, I was always an outsider—even to my close friends. The history of Black-White hatred separated us. They, as well as I, felt the need to constantly verbalize that we were friends *in spite* of the racism that exists between Blacks and Whites. Cultural differences also underlined our separateness. I dressed in casual clothes—Levi's and a sport shirt—but these were different from the clothes worn by Vice Lords; I was not conversant in street slang; and I did not act properly in certain social situations. This last factor was especially important. For example, one evening I was in a bar with Sonny. We were standing together talking when three attractive girls walked by. Sonny shook his head slowly and said, "Foxes! Stone Foxes!" [A "fox" is an attractive girl. A "stone fox" is an extremely attractive girl.] I laughed and raised my hand to slap him on the shoulder. In the ghetto there is a particular way people express agreement. This is what I have called "hand slapping" in *The Vice Lords* and Blacks generally call it "slapping fine." This custom has now begun to diffuse to Whites, but at the time, it was not generally known outside the ghetto. If A says something felt by B to be worth emphasizing, B will raise his hand. A will then put out his hand palm up, and B will slap it. Now when I raised my hand to slap Sonny on the shoulder, I was initiating an action that was both very similar, if not identical, to the beginning moves of a hand-slapping episode, and occurred in a context that was grammatical for such an episode. Therefore, without thinking, Sonny put out his hand palm up. However, as soon as he did so, he realized that I was White, and did not customarily emphasize agreement in this manner. At the same time, I knew about hand slapping, and understood what Sonny was doing. For an instant we were staring at each other—Sonny with his hand out, but making motions to drop it, and me with my hand raised in the air. Sonny did not know whether to drop his hand or not, and I did not know if I should slap his hand or his shoulder. I decided to slap his hand at the same time he decided to put it down. We both laughed with embarrassment and shook our heads. But the ease of the moment had been lost, and the Black-White gulf that separated us was brought sharply into focus. Anthropologists often have experiences like this in their work with alien cultures, but in this case the incident had extra significance because of the history of Black-White relations in the United States. It emphasized that we were from two different cultures, but it also emphasized that we were from two groups of people who had a long history of hatred and suppression between them. Elliot Liebow in *Tally's Corner* uses the particularly apt metaphor of a linked fence to express this separation. According to Liebow, he and his Black informants could walk along together, see each other, and even occasionally touch, but the fence remained between them (Liebow 1967:250–251).

Ways of recording data are another facet of the methods problem. Each evening I wrote as much of my observations as could be remembered. It would have been best to have carried a small notebook with me so that I could have taken notes on the spot. Initially I did this, but it made most Vice Lords so uneasy for me to take out my notebook and write down something that I decided to stop. Further, much of the social interaction between Vice Lords that I observed occurred while individuals were riding in my car and could not be written in my notebook at the time. I attempted to remember as much as possible, but at the end of the day I always knew that much had been forgotten.

Interviews with various informants were another source of data. I conducted structured interviews and gathered life histories. A tape-recorder was used to record this material. There are difficulties in using a tape-recorder, but I felt the advantages easily outweighed the disadvantages. I was able to record highly detailed accounts of interviews that I could not have written by hand. Transcribing the tapes was the main difficulty. It took me months of steady work to finish the transcriptions. My research took three months of one summer and one month of another, but if it had taken an entire year—usually the minimum time an anthropologist spends in the field—the task of transcribing the tapes would have been monumental.

In recording life histories I simply asked the informant to tell about his life. The only questions asked were either those necessary to clarify something I did not understand or those necessary to get further amplification of an incident I felt was interesting and important. Structured interviews were organized around particular topics. These were derived primarily from my observations. If I thought something I had observed needed amplification, I focused on this in a structured interview. For example, I had heard Vice Lords refer to their "territory." References were made both to the territory of the branch, and to the territories of particular sections. This suggested the following questions: how are the territories of particular branches distinguished from one another, and from those of rival clubs; and what distinguishes the territories of sections? From putting together data gathered from observations, I was able to get an answer to the first question. I had no clue, however, to the way section territories were distinguished, and so I focused on this problem in a series of structured interviews.

It will be useful to include some of these interviews in this chapter because they illustrate one of the biggest difficulties in conducting structured interviews. This is the problem of framing the right questions to ask an informant. The anthropologist really has to know what kind of answers will be correct before he can think up questions that will elicit what he wants to know. In the example above, I wanted to know how section territories were distinguished. I thought that sections must hold different rights in particular parts of Vice Lord City and so I framed my questions in these terms. This idea was wrong. Therefore, the questions I asked failed to get me closer to understanding the basis for the distinction. My first interview was with a Vice Lord known as Duck. It went as follows:

R.L.K. What's the territory of the Ridgeway Lords?

Duck Ridgeway, all the way from 18th to Independence.

R.L.K. Where do most of the Ridgeway Lords hang out?

Duck On 16th Street. There be very few on Ridgeway.

R.L.K. If they all hang out on 16th Street, why aren't they considered 16th Street Lords?

Duck 16th Street just a hang out for everybody.

R.L.K. When you say that's the territory of the Ridgeway Lords, what do you mean? What does it mean that you have that territory?

Duck Everybody got their little section where they hang out at. It's just different street names. They just go by street names, that's all.

R.L.K. Well, is it because they live on that street, or is it because they hang out on that street?

Duck They hang out on that street, and most of them live on the street, but you don't have to live on the street.

R.L.K. O.K., suppose you live on Ridgeway, and you're in the Ridgeway Lords, and you move away, does that change your membership, or can you still belong?

Duck You can still belong.

R.L.K. But if you start hanging around with the group where you live now will that change your membership?

Duck Not exactly. I keep telling you we all the same. You can belong to one group, but you can hang out wherever you want.

It was obvious I was no closer to understanding the basis for section territorial distinctions than before I started the interview. But I still failed to realize that my questions were based on an incorrect assumption about what the right answers might be, and in the next interview I worked from the same direction. Therefore, I not only missed an important clue, but also thought I found the basis for the distinction which was, in fact, not the case at all.

R.L.K. As a member of the Ridgeway Lords, what is the difference between my territory and your territory?

Earl They trying to keep the Roman Saints from falling down on us, and we trying to keep the Cobras from falling down on them. We got two different groups coming from two different ways. From the east it's the Roman Saints, and from the west it's the Cobras. We trying to hold the Cobras back far as we can so they won't get closer to 16th and Lawndale, 'cause 15th Street is the back door to the City.

R.L.K.   What I'm trying to get at is what difference having a particular territory means for individuals in different groups. Now I don't know if this is the case, but are there certain things that Ridgeway Lords can do in their territory that they can't do in your territory?

Earl   You right there. Like some of the 15th Street Lords might go over there—they ain't got no business jumping on no one over there, and they ain't got no business coming over to our hood and jumping on somebody.

The first answer should have given me a clue as to how Vice Lords distinguish between section territories, but because I assumed there must be differences in terms of rights, I failed to see its significance. When I asked Earl to give me an answer in terms of rights, he did. This simply led me further along a blind alley. It was not until the interview with Big Otis that I finally understood the basis for territorial distinctions between sections. I started this interview with the same assumption. Fortunately Goliath was present. He saw at once what I was trying to find out, and why I was getting nowhere. Goliath provided the right questions to ask as well as the right answers.

Goliath   What advantages do you have in your own territory?

Big Otis We know all the gangways and rooftops, and we know just about everybody in the streets.

Goliath   Do you use your territory also like a meeting place? Like for instance, all the fellows get together to go someplace and take care of business (get together for a raid on an enemy club), could you all meet in this same area, could you get together right away, like could you contact everybody?

Big Otis Yeah, you know where to find them at. You know where all the places they be at.

Goliath   In other words, you wouldn't have to worry about the Cobras coming down and whupping you in you territory.

Big Otis No, we know it before they get down there.

R.L.K.   How is this different from the territory of the Ridgeway Lords?

Big Otis It's no different.

R.L.K.   Why isn't the territory of the Ridgeway Lords your territory? What makes it different?

Goliath   See, everybody in one box, like for instance Tex and them, they be on 15th Street, so they make sure don't nobody come down Ridgeway that we don't know. This way you block off the whole area, and there always be somebody around. If you can't handle it, then you get help.

Big Otis Yeah, if the Cobras coming from one end and the Saints coming from another, it's our job on 15th Street to stop the Cobras.

It is apparent that the distinction between section territories is based on differential responsibility rather than differential rights. Sections have the re-

A Vice Lord corner.

sponsibility for protecting particular parts of Vice Lord City from enemy attacks. A section's territory, therefore, is that part of Vice Lord City for which it is responsible in case of enemy attack. In order to fulfill this responsibility, section members must have good knowledge of how their territory is laid out— where gangways lead, how to gain access to rooftops, what alleys are deadends, and the like. It is advantageous, if not necessary, to have such knowledge when section members must actually defend their territory against enemy raids. While sections have the duty to defend a particular part of Vice Lord City, they have the right to assistance from other Vice Lord groups if they can not accomplish this alone. It is the duty, however, that is crucial in differentiating section territories.

Another aspect of the data-gathering problem stems from the theoretical orientation of the researcher. "Facts" are intimately connected with theory. What I saw as facts and therefore recorded, was directly related to my theoretical orientation. Because of my orientation, I did not record certain things that are undoubtedly important.

My theoretical orientation was that of a social anthropologist. In social anthropology human behavior is generally looked at from the perspective of social interaction. The concept of culture is important too, but is important primarily as it relates to social interaction. The basic postulate on which social anthropology rests is that social interaction is not random but has an order to it. In other words, social life forms a system. When looking at social interaction as a system, social anthropologists often employ the ideas of social groups, and social roles in getting at patterns and regularities. It is much more complicated than this, but what I have described is basic to what social anthropologists do. In any case, it was this orientation that directed my research; the questions that I asked and the data that I recorded were dictated by it.

But I did not ask other important questions and collect other important data. For example, I did not look at Vice Lord behavior in terms of social networks. After becoming acquainted with the network idea, it was evident that certain aspects of Vice Lord life would have made better sense if ordered in terms of this idea. I had not thought in terms of social networks, however, and therefore had not collected the necessary data.[1] Other anthropologists with different basic orientations would undoubtedly have asked yet again different questions, collected different data, and arrived at different pictures of Vice Lord life.

The Problem of Emotional Reactions

One of the greatest difficulties in my Vice Lord research was handling my emotional responses. On the streets of the ghetto I was functionally an infant, and like all infants, had to be taken care of. I did not know what was, and what was not, potentially dangerous; and I did not understand the significance of most actions and many words. For example, one afternoon while I was standing on 15th Street with a group of Vice Lords, a young man in his early twenties walked up and started yelling that he was a Roman Saint, and was going to "whup" every Vice Lord he found. It was obvious by the way he talked and acted that he was mentally deranged. One of the Vice Lords said, "The dude's crazy, Man! He ain't no Saint. Leave him alone." Suddenly a dead-pan look came over the young man's face. Abruptly he turned from us, and walked down an alley that was directly opposite from where we were standing. Very calmly, and with no show of speed, every Vice Lord in the group walked away, out of a line of possible fire. Suddenly I found myself standing alone, looking down the alley at this fellow. Tex came up and pulled me to the side. He said, "Man, the dude get to the end of the alley, he liable to get his jive together and burn you down (pull out his gun and shoot you)!" Besides feeling stupid, I did not know whether to be afraid or not. The fellow reached the end of the alley, turned the corner, and was gone. The extent of my helplessness had been made quite clear.

When you are an infant in age, it is one thing to be helpless, but when you

---

[1] Social networks are the web of social ties built up by individuals mainly on a personal basis. See "Theoretical Orientations in African Urban Studies" (Mitchell 1966), "The Significance of Quasi-Groups in the Study of Complex Societies" (Mayer 1966), and especially, "Networks and Political Process" (Barnes 1968) for a discussion in depth of the notion of social network, and its importance for urban research.

are twenty-nine years old, it is quite something else. This feeling of helplessness was very difficult for me to handle. In the early part of my research it often made me feel so nervous and anxious that the events occurring around me seemed to merge in a blur of meaningless action. I despaired of ever making any sense out of anything. Vice Lords sensed my feelings and I could see it made some people uncomfortable. This increased the difficulty of gaining the rapport necessary to carry out successful research.

The only solution to this problem was not to give up. Slowly the weeks passed, and as I became more familiar with the members of the club and the neighborhood, this feeling subsided. And then, suddenly I started understanding things. But although I may no longer have been an infant, I was still a child. Whenever I thought I was really "hip," that I really "knew what was happening," something would occur that brought home the extent of my ignorance. For example, on the very last night of my first summer's field work I mistook a challenge to fight for a friendly warning. A Vice Lord said to me, "Hey man, you better walk light!" Because a gang fight had taken place a few hours earlier, and because I had heard "walk light" used in previous contexts as a friendly warning, I completely misunderstood and responded most inappropriately, "Yeah, I'm hip." Actually I could not have been more unhip for "You walk light!" or "You better walk light!" is usually a challenge to fight, while simply "Walk light!" is used as a friendly warning. Because of the complete inappropriateness of my response, my would-be protagonist did not know how to proceed. He stood there for a minute, and then walked across the street and attempted to get other Vice Lords to support him in attacking me. Goliath, however, went over and started threatening him, and an argument ensued. Finally, after it was apparent that no one would follow him in "jumping on" me, and some would actively oppose him, he left the corner. I did not find out what had taken place until later when I asked Goliath what the argument across the street had been about.

I also had emotional responses to events that stemmed from my own value system. How to handle these responses was another source of difficulty. There were certain aspects of Vice Lord life—and I need not go into them—that I found personally distasteful. In the early part of my research, they made me upset and uneasy. Later, at times I found myself getting angry. Although intellectually I felt my values were not demonstrably superior, I still could not stop my emotional reactions. These reactions often made it difficult for me to retain objectivity. More important, I was never completely sure if Vice Lords sensed my reactions, and in turn reacted to them. Thus I was not always certain if my feelings affected the events I was trying to observe. Although I tried to control my responses as much as possible, I am still not sure how successful I was. Undoubtedly some bias crept into my observations, and probably certain events I was trying to observe were changed in subtle ways in response to my emotional reactions.

The Problem of Writing Up the Data

Writing up data into some kind of coherent account involves at least two problems. First, the anthropologist must decide on the data to be included in the work, and second, he must decide on the manner in which to organize and present the data that is included. The first problem is often difficult to solve because in writing an account it is necessary to describe living people, many of whom are close friends. This is especially difficult when the study may be read by members of the society in which it was carried out, as was the case with *The Vice Lords* (Keiser, 1969). I think most anthropologists feel an obligation to write nothing that could injure the people in the group in which they worked. On the other hand, the anthropologist wants to write the best possible account he can, and information that members of a society might not want known can be important for understanding how particular social and cultural systems work. If information was given in confidence, then the anthropologist has the moral obligation to keep that confidence. In other instances the anthropologist may have information not given in confidence that people still might not want others to know about. One obvious solution is to change names, dates, and places so that the description cannot be linked to particular people. Sometimes, however, changes such as these will not provide an adequate disguise. Then, in my opinion, the particular information should not be included if it is really injurious to the people involved. The difficulty comes in deciding whether something is really injurious. I do not think there is any simple, clear-cut answer to this problem. The anthropologist must be as sensitive as possible to the feelings and problems of the people he is describing, and write his account accordingly.

In trying to solve the second problem, that of organization and presentation, my theoretical orientation was as important as it was in gathering the data. The theoretical orientation provided a framework on which I tried to construct a coherent account. My main goal was to demonstrate the systematic nature of Vice Lord social life. In order to do this, however, it was necessary to take a cultural perspective as well, for aspects of culture related to patterns of social interaction in important ways. I started with definitions of the cultural and social systems. The social system was defined as the ordered system of on-going social interaction; and the cultural system as the ordered system of beliefs and values in terms of which social interaction takes place.

After an introductory chapter tracing out general lines of Vice Lord development, I described certain features of Vice Lord social structure. This included such things as the series of groups to which Vice Lords belong, the set of political offices that are held by particular members, and the way the club relates to physical space. It was necessary to describe these aspects first so the reader could follow the later argument. In the following two chapters I tried to show that part of the pattern and order in Vice Lord social life was in the systematic relationship of social groups and social roles to recurring sets of behavior recognized by Vice Lords as forming distinct social contexts. In these two chapters my argument was based on three crucial ideas—social groups, social roles, and social contexts. These ideas formed an important part of the framework around which I organized my material. The idea of social contexts was especially important since it was the relationship of groups and roles to particular social contexts that was patterned and ordered. Here is where the cultural system became crucial. The social contexts were differentiated from one another in terms of beliefs and values that formed part of the Vice Lord cultural system, and in the next chapter I discussed some of these. Thus the set of social contexts that gave order to social roles and social groups was in turn ordered by the beliefs and values of the Vice Lord cultural system. The final chapter was an edited version of a life history. It was included to give the reader a different perspective on Vice Lord life than the one provided by the more formal account of earlier chapters. I hoped by including all this material and organizing it in this manner that the reader would gain some idea of the nature of Vice Lord life.

References

Banton, Michael, 1957, West African City. London: Oxford University Press, for the International African Institute.

Barnes, J. A., 1968, Networks and Political Process. In Marc J. Swartz, ed., Local-Level Politics. Chicago: Aldine.

Keiser, R. Lincoln, 1969, The Vice Lords: Warriors of the Streets. New York: Holt, Rinehart and Winston, Inc.

Liebow, Elliot, 1967, Tally's Corner. Boston: Little, Brown and Company.

Mayer, Adrian C., 1966, The Significance of Quasi-Groups in the Study of Complex Societies. In Michael Banton, ed., The Social Anthropology of Complex Societies. A.S.A. Monographs No. 4. London: Tavistock.

Mitchell, J. Clyde, 1966, Theoretical Orientations in African Urban Studies. In Michael Banton, ed., The Social Anthropology of Complex Societies. A.S.A. Monographs No. 4. London: Tavistock.

Short, James F., Jr., and Fred L. Strodtbeck, 1965, Group Process and Gang Delinquency. Chicago: University of Chicago Press.

Conclusion

THE PURPOSE OF THIS BOOK has been to provide a systematic description of the Vice Lord way of life. In contructing this description certain concepts have been used as an organizing framework. These concepts provided perspectives for the study of Vice Lord behavior. First, we looked at the Vice Lord world in terms of a social system, and analyzed patterns in social interaction. We also studied Vice Lord behavior in terms of ideological sets which functioned both to divide Vice Lord reality into segments and to guide and judge behavior within these segments. Finally, we viewed the Vice Lord way of life through the eyes of an actual participant by means of an autobiographical life history.

Our description, however, is not complete, and further research is needed. The analysis of roles is a case in point. There is a social identity "partner" that seems to be important in political alliances. In some ways it appears similar to the identity Vice Lord, but further information is lacking. The roles comprised of male-female identities are also a blank spot in the description. Another area that needs more research is political dynamics. A detailed study of friendship networks showing the distribution of friendship ties would help us better understand the way political alliances crystallize. We should also note that the Vice Lords are a part of the Black ghetto, and we need to know how the Vice Lord social and cultural systems are related to those of the Black community. Finally, a detailed comparative study of a number of clubs like the Vice Lords would help us better understand why such groups develop in the particular ways they do.

References for the
Case Study

GEERTZ, C., 1957, "Ritual and Social Change: A Javanese Example," *American Anthropologist,* Vol. 59, No. 1.

HOBEN, A., N.D., *Community Study Guide,* a mimeographed pamphlet for Peace Corps Volunteers in Ethiopia.

KEIL, C., 1966, *The Urban Blues.* Chicago: University of Chicago Press.

SHORT, J. JR., 1963, "Introduction to the Abridged Edition," in *The Gang* by Frederic M. Thrasher. Chicago: University of Chicago Press.

Recommended Readings

BROWN, C., 1965, *Manchild in the Promised Land,* New York: Macmillan. An autobiographical account of ghetto life in Harlem. Brown tells about such things as his family, his gang-fighting experiences, and his encounters with narcotics. *Manchild* provides a wealth of ethnographic details on ghetto culture.

HORTON, J., 1967, "Time and Cool People," *Trans-action,* Vol. 4, No. 5 (April). An excellent analysis of time concepts in Black ghetto culture by a sociologist. Horton based his study on field research carried out in a Los Angeles ghetto area.

KEIL, C., 1966, *The Urban Blues.* Chicago: The University of Chicago Press. A fascinating analysis of Black ghetto music in its cultural and social contexts. Keil's work is based on data collected through first-hand field research. He analyzes blues not only as music, but also as a cultural pattern that has ramifications throughout the ghetto cultural and social systems. *The Urban Blues,* with its emphasis on understanding ghetto life in its own right, provides a much needed counter-balance to the "deviancy" orientation of much of the current social science literature dealing with the Black ghetto.

LEIBOW, E., 1967, *Tally's Corner: A Study of Negro Streetcorner Men.* Boston, Mass.: Little, Brown. An anthropologist's interesting and penetrating account of Black street-corner life in Washington, D.C. Leibow's conclusion that the distinctive aspects of ghetto behavior are not the manifestations of an independent cultural tradition, but the failure to achieve the goals of the larger society has interesting implications.

SHORT, J. JR., AND STRODTBECK, F., 1965, *Group Process and Gang Delinquency.* Chicago: The University of Chicago Press.

A collection of recent articles illustrating the concern with deviancy found in much of the sociological literature on fighting clubs. The data on which the authors base their analysis comes from fighting clubs of Chicago, including the Vice Lords.

THRASHER, F., 1927, abridged ed. 1963, *The Gang.* Chicago: University of Chicago Press.

An early study of youth gangs by one of the most important members of the "Chicago School" of sociology.

WHYTE, W., 1943, *Street Corner Society.* Chicago: The University of Chicago Press.

A study of a street-corner group by a scholar who conducted actual anthropological field research. Whyte's analysis of the social structure of an Italian slum community is a classic in the field of urban studies.

WILLIAMSON, H., 1966, *Hustler! The Autobiography of a Thief.* R. Lincoln Keiser, ed. New York: Doubleday.

A life history of a hustler in Chicago's South Side Black ghetto. Williamson belonged to a fighting club in his early teens, but soon graduated to a career of hustling.

YABLONSKY, L., 1962, *The Violent Gang.* New York: Macmillan.

The literature on the sociology of fighting clubs is truly voluminous. Yablonsky's work is a good starting point for those interested in the sociological approach since it provides capsule versions of major theories of gang delinquency.